The Life of Thomas Cranmer

THE LIFE OF
THOMAS CRANMER

THEODORE MAYNARD

HENRY REGNERY COMPANY
Chicago   *1956*

In Memoriam

Charles Williams

Introduction

It is well-known that a man on intimate terms with the Catholic priesthood—whether he himself be a priest or only a layman—sometimes encounters a poor shabby man in lay attire and instantly recognizes him as a priest. This has never actually happened to me, and certainly Thomas Cranmer himself was no clerical "bum" in disguise, but I am sure that had I met him in the circumstances just described, I would, after a few minutes, have known that he was a priest—and not from any spoken word but from the expression of his features. Under the big, rather straggly beard that he wore after the death of Henry VIII, by way of expressing his unending grief that his friend was no more, it may be that his disguise would have been almost impenetrable. But the fine painting of the clean-shaven Thomas Cranmer that hangs in the National Portrait Gallery in London makes clear what I mean. The man depicted is a priest and could not be mistaken for anything else.

Yet what kind of priest? No reflection is intended upon Cranmer's moral character to say that he did not receive ordination until relatively late in life (for that not infrequently happened in those days, just as the contrary—ordination before the canonical age—was common enough) but it merely indicates that Cranmer took his coloration from the clerical society in which he had lived from adolescence. I must conclude that it was from this that he derived his unmistakable stamp, though without ever giving the sign, so far as we know, that he had the clerical vocation. There can be no question that he had the outward marks of a priest, quite apart from whether or not he had the priest's interior disposition.

What are the marks that I have in mind? Some of the anticlerical sort might use the words "sleekness" or "smugness." These words might fit Cranmer's portrait, but they are not generally applicable; "constraint" might be better. Yet I, who have known intimately a great many priests, would not consider any of these terms exactly right. All that I am prepared to say is that sometimes too close a preoccupation with his profession may give a man away, but that this preoccupation, when it exists, is most likely to be found among the less warm-hearted priests, that is, among those who play a role with too much self-consciousness. The rest, the vast majority, are natural and at ease, though perhaps some of them are inclined to be a bit guarded until they are sure of the company they are in. But Thomas Cranmer *always* seemed to be constrained and self-conscious—perhaps, it should be said, "too parsonical." One might almost read the whole history of the Church of England "as by law established" written upon his face!

This may provoke the rejoinder that many Catholic priests of England and America possess a physiognomy in which we may discern too plainly the map of Ireland. If so, I much prefer this to the other thing. For though I have been sometimes accused— on no grounds that I know of except my English birth—of being anti-Irish, actually I am, if anything, too violently pro-Irish. But this much I will admit: I like best a Catholic priest who sinks his nationality in his office, as all except a few do. The point I am making is that Thomas Cranmer was too much an *English* parson; just look at that painting of him! But if he was parsonical, I fear that it was because he had acquired the cast of countenance without having strong religious convictions; he was not enough of a priest of God.

There are relatively few lives of Cranmer, though of course he figures largely in all the histories of his period, especially in the biographies of Henry VIII, one of the most luridly gorgeous persons any writer could wish to have as a subject, even if one of them dismisses him, as did Charles Dickens, as a blot of blood and grease upon an otherwise glorious volume. You will get, for instance, some part of him in Fuller, and Burnet and Lingard, but Strype was almost the first person to write about him *in extenso,* though this consisted mainly in gathering the germane documents, which were essential for the later, more thorough-going biographers. Of these the best, in my estimation, are Henry John Todd, who published his study in two volumes in 1831, and Professor Pollard, whose single volume came out in 1905. Pollard has the advantage of being a trained historian and uses his materials well, but he is inferior to Todd in the account he gives of Cranmer's trial at Oxford. Both are definitely on the Protestant side.

As definitely on the Catholic side, but a much more vivid writer, is Hilaire Belloc, whose *Cranmer* was issued in 1931. But as one who knew Mr. Belloc and owes a good deal to him in many ways, I have to record my regretful opinion that, despite his brilliant literary style, he was not merely prejudiced (for that might be pardoned) but also monstrously unfair. He says that he based his work upon Pollard—though that basis is not very apparent, except where it does not greatly matter—but that he set out to produce not so much a biography, as an exposition of Cranmer's character and motives, with special emphasis upon the man's literary genius. Considered as a literary appraisal, Belloc's book is probably better than any of the others, as may also be true of his Milton, for here, again, he is better equipped than anybody else. These aspects of Cranmer he draws out most effectively, but I must say that I think him often wide of the mark when he delineates Cranmer's character and motives. Yet he is able to correct Pollard on a few important facts, and I have been glad to make use of some—but only some—of the Bellocian Catholic strength. His main weakness is that he has manifestly not read much of Cranmer's writings and so is unaware that the man's thought developed very slowly. In general he represents Cranmer as hypocritically posing as a Catholic in subservience to Henry VIII, as long as Henry was alive, and then of throwing off the mask the moment Edward VI ascended the throne.

The fact is, however, that Cranmer's mode of thinking changed more than once, even under Edward. Belloc leaves out of account that Cranmer's views on a number of subjects did undergo such a change—largely under the influence of the foreign theologians who began to arrive in England, leaving their imprint on the Book of Common Prayer and, even more, upon the new code of Canon Law he was about to ask Convocation and Parliament to pass. If this code had little chance of becoming statutory law, this was because of the personal antipathy that the new dictator, the Duke of Northumberland, felt towards the Archbishop of Canterbury, and because the Duke did not wish to confuse his main project with what was, to him, a side issue.

Cranmer is usually thought of as a mild man, and to do him

justice, he would probably have remained mild. He did little real leading throughout life, but was amenable to the molding his mind received from others. At all events he was not very mild in the new code of Canon Law foreign fanatics wished him to introduce, for under their guidance he was ready to ask that the death penalty—which meant, of course, by burning—be inflicted on those who believed in Transubstantiation. This was in line with what people believed everywhere, and Cranmer may not have intended more than something to be held *in terrorem,* as even Henry VIII did with regard to his Act of Six Articles, except occasionally. But it should be remembered of Cranmer.

Belloc attacks the surreptitious introduction of the Tyndale version while Henry was still King, and in terms which almost suggest that Belloc hated the vernacular version of the Scriptures, whereas he should have confined himself to saying that what Cranmer (in conjunction with Cromwell) did was exceedingly tricky. In this we see an even more un-Catholic frame of mind than that expressed in Belloc's famous formula: "The Faith is Europe and Europe is the Faith."

But perhaps I am now being unfair in my turn. We all know that the versatile Belloc had a number of crotchets. While I feel sure that he is often mistaken, all English-speaking Catholics are heavily in his debt, and none more so than myself. Even though I am obliged to dissent from some of the conclusions in his *Cranmer,* for his work as a whole I have the utmost admiration, especially for his satires, and of these most of all for his masterpiece, *The Mercy of Allah.* In advance I announce that my *Life of Thomas Cranmer* will not begin to equal his in power of writing. I will do my poor best, but can only undertake to be more fair.

This does not mean that I like Cranmer very much, though with very few exceptions he was well liked. Mine is an extremely difficult task: that of presenting a strangely complex character, who was looked upon as simple and mild in his own time. Possibly he would have been that, if only he could have been left alone. But in the position into which he was forced by circumstances, there was nothing except to use simplicity and mildness to conceal devious objectives. I shall make no defense of him, but I do object to defamation, though there are three or four occasions when I deplore his conduct. But it may be said for him that he had little choice and so cannot be held as primarily guilty. It is in a spirit of pity that I write.

As I have had to condemn some elements in Belloc's study, I add that John Lingard followed a policy of "leaning backwards" —as otherwise he would not have obtained a hearing. His policy justified itself, and he is read even today, defective though his documentation was. But the Protestant William Cobbett bellowed at the top of his voice what Lingard said so moderately, and therefore is held in unwarranted disesteem. His religion was of a political sort, as he records an English parson saying to him: his intention was to show the English peasantry how they had been plundered. He was right, but that is not the whole story. Cranmer resisted, so far as lay within his power, the exploitation of the poor. If he showed little (being unable to show much) concern about Henry's looting of the monasteries, he did what he could to prevent the looting of chantries and guilds and schools. He was not very effective, but no ecclesiastic could do much against the gang operating under the Duke of Somerset and the Duke of Northumberland. His protests deserve to be remembered.

The two best writers upon Cranmer's period are Father Philip Hughes with his three volumes, and the Frenchman, G. Constant, with his two. But both are historians rather than biographers, even though they introduce many vivid vignettes of personalities into their work, as these are indispensable to the student of the times. I mention only Catholic writers, as I may have dealt rather severely with Belloc. But of course there are many non-Catholic writers who are very good, though in my estimation none quite comes up to these. The explanation may be that all—Catholic or Protestant—are a bit afraid of tackling Thomas Cranmer, and that one has to be very bold (or very foolish) to present Cranmer as a Protestant hero, as might be possible with Martin Luther. For their part, Catholic writers are not very anxious to get into what might prove to be acrimonious controversy.

Thomas Cranmer's mind, I repeat, was not much inclined to strike out boldly on its own account, but was nearly always one that followed rather than blazed trails. Belloc presupposes that the mind of a man nearing forty is so fixed that further development is impossible. In general this may be true, but he forgets that Cranmer was inordinately slow and cautious, even for a middle-aged university Don. By sheer accident released from the Cambridge routine—which was not until he had just turned forty—he could not easily have adjusted himself at first to the new world of great people. Until that time he had lived secluded, and if previously little eddies of thought had swirled round him, these had not in the least affected him. Suddenly dragged out upon a great stage it must have been some time before he could overcome his habits of settled somnolence, or, if you like, from the academic scholasticism which appears to have been at that time somewhat dull and deadening. It may not have been until he was at last sent abroad on official business that he discovered this to be a new world, though he still did not guess the part he was destined to play in it. Then gradually a different Cranmer emerged, one still deferential and courteous, as he was even in the trial, still so many years away, that sent him to the stake, but a Cranmer whose torpid mind had begun to quicken, without his suspecting where he would at last arrive.

Yet those sproutings of his mind may have been all the more strong and stubborn when they eventually appeared above ground. This explains, I think, why his many recantations before he was burned at the stake were not really recantations at all, for every one of them, while attempting some improvement upon the one written just before, used some phrase or other to show that, willing as he was to submit to royal authority, he would not whole-heartedly submit to the authority of the Pope.

One must admire such fidelity to a belatedly reached principle, however misguided one may think it. His reluctance to surrender in such an awful crisis suggests what the young university Don must have been, beating his syllogisms into the heads of his Cambridge students. Yet such fancies are beside the point: Thomas Cranmer in Oxford in 1555 stuck to his guns, conceding all that he could concede, but yielding nothing that was essential.

And he knew quite well what the outcome must be, though no doubt he hoped to the end that the last grudgingly spoken word would prove to be enough. When he came to see that in this he was mistaken, he went out defiantly to a martyr's death at the stake.

THEODORE MAYNARD

Contents

Chapter One

Early Years

As is so often the case with those destined to become very famous, but whose subsequent fame was quite unlooked for, we do not know a great deal about the early life of Thomas Cranmer, though as is also often true, we have somewhat fuller information than might be expected, most of it coming from Cranmer himself. We know that his early life followed a pattern with which we are fairly familiar, that of a younger son in the family of a minor country squire and, a few years later, that of a university student. If there is not a great deal of a positive sort to relate, this is chiefly because the facts are not of a very exciting kind. The day by day routine is hardly worth recording, because it is so decorous and dull. Though that in itself might carry grist to another mill, I beg to be excused; partly because I do not wish to use fictional embellishment, and also because we know fairly well what kind of people the Cranmers were and what part, in particular, Thomas Cranmer played among them. The flat mediocrity should be stressed plainly and strongly, for it is strange that from such a family—especially in an age when social standing and powerful patrons counted for so much—this man, in middle age, suddenly emerged into eminence. This must have been surprising to all his acquaintances, and surprising even to himself.

No doubt those who live in the English Midlands would resent—and quite understandably—a description of their part of the country as uninteresting. But it might be allowed to pass without offense if one adds that, while it contains a number of pretty villages, the landscape itself is, compared to the rich variety of some other parts of England, rather monotonous. Running down the middle of northern England, and inclining somewhat to the west as it proceeds, is the only English mountain chain, dividing Yorkshire and Lancashire rather sharply from one another. In the southeast, chiefly in the county of Sussex, stretches another range which can be called mountains only by a stretch of the imagination—indeed they are hardly high enough to be called hills. These are the South Downs, and they seem more like breast-works than anything else. Belloc in his fine poem "The South Country" finds the exact words for them: "So noble and so bare." But as they straggle into the adjoining counties of Kent and Hampshire, they provide rolling hills of considerable charm. Rather oddly, twenty or thirty miles away are the North Downs, which are more thickly wooded but even lower. Their charm is somewhat different. Then the whole of the Thames valley is one of the loveliest things in the world, for along it on either side rise small hills abundant in verdure wherever the river makes its winding way, and much the same must be said of the other river valleys of England. None of them, however, approach the incomparable beauty of the Thames until one reaches the Severn, which marks the beginning of Wales, a mountainous country but one in which the mountains are seldom lofty. There are other hilly ranges—the Cotswolds and the Chilterns —but they are accounted such only out of local patriotism, being clumps rather than ranges. Cornwall is very rocky, and this might also be said of bleak Dartmoor. The rockiness extends, though lessening by degrees, into Wiltshire and

Dorset. The whole of the south coast has chalk cliffs, with stony cliffs in Cornwall and much of Yorkshire, all the way to Scotland. The east coast, on the other hand—roughly from the estuary of the Humber to the estuary of the Thames—is low-lying and reminds one of Holland at times, its main feature being the large indentation known as the Wash.

My intention is not to attempt any detailed description of the physical formation of England, especially since it is so varied; I touch on the matter only because landscape does affect the mind and character. We should therefore try to picture the part of the country where Cranmer was born and where he spent his childhood.

Thomas Cranmer's birthplace was Aslacton, a hamlet so small it is not shown on any ordinary map. It lay perhaps thirty miles due west of the Wash, with Nottingham not much further inland and Newark due north. The easiest way to place it might be to look for Grantham, but the railway line connecting Newark and Grantham does not pass through Aslacton, and before there was any railway, the Fosse Way, the main means of travel between London and Yorkshire, did not touch the hamlet, so that the very few people who had occasion to go there, had to leave the high road and go to their destination by a rough road that was little more than a track.

As the land was flat, on a clear day one could make out the mass of Nottingham Castle, though the town of Nottingham was a place the Cranmers very rarely visited. As even the first hedges had only recently been planted to divide field from field, the vista was almost unbroken. But Sherwood Forest, that tract celebrated in legend and ballad more than it should be, was near at hand, and though it had never been so thickly wooded as its name suggests—not

3

even in the days of the fabulous Robin Hood—most of the trees there had been cut down by the sixteenth century; at all events there were not enough of them to impede the eye. Although clumps of trees stood here and there, and at this point or that a church spire, it was upon an almost level plain that the Cranmers looked out. The houses of the more well-to-do were fairly substantially built; those of the poor were usually only thatched. They would have seemed picturesque, except that the people of Aslacton took them, as they took their dark discomfort, for granted.

If one traveled through Sherwood Forest one came at the end of the day's ride to the famous Welbeck Abbey. It had been remodeled or added to so often that it bore little resemblance to what it formerly was, and of course it was expropriated in 1539 by Henry VIII and is now the seat of the Duke of Portland. It is significant to us that in Cranmer's time the Abbot of Welbeck had most of the local ecclesiastical livings in his gift, so that the priest at Aslacton was there by his appointment. It seems just a little strange that young Cranmer, when he (or rather his widowed mother) decided that he should seek his livelihood in the Church, did not become one of the monks (or rather canons) of Welbeck.

This abbey was the head of thirty-five houses of the English Premonstratensians, an offshoot of the Augustinian Canons, founded in the twelfth century by St. Norbert for the special purpose of preaching. The Order was, however, somewhat diverted from its original purpose by falling unduly under the influence of the Cistercians, who, like other Benedictines, kept to the cloister. They lived like monks, and were nearly lost sight of in the preponderance of Benedictines, whereas had St. Norbert's plans been fully carried out,

4

the Premonstratensians might have anticipated the work of the friars of the thirteenth century. Nevertheless, Welbeck Abbey, in wealth and splendor, had become one of the great religious houses. Thomas Cranmer may be said to have grown up under its shadow. If he did not join the community, the guess might be hazarded that this was because the Cranmer family was not wealthy enough to offer what the Abbey expected from a newly admitted novice.

Thomas Cranmer the elder, who was born about the middle of the fifteenth century, was one of the lesser gentry but was entitled to a coat-of-arms—three cranes. This was a kind of pun upon the family name: "Crane Mere." This Cranmer married a woman of at least equal social standing but of no great wealth. She was Agnes Hatfield of Willoughby near Nottingham. By the marriage three boys and at least four girls were born. One of the daughters later came to be suspected of bigamy, a crime which was not very uncommon in those days and which could usually be kept hidden by the simple expedient of moving to a locality where one's antecedents were unknown. However, the fact did not come to light until Archbishop Cranmer had found some enemies, when it furnished ammunition to the Prebendaries of Canterbury Cathedral who, late in Henry VIII's reign, were lodging complaints against one suspected of heretical leanings.

It is not necessary to linger upon Cranmer's sisters, since little about them is known, and most of that little is good, except for the scandal just mentioned, if it was really proved. Only the sons of the family need concern us. The Squire's eldest son was of course to inherit the estate, so the two remaining sons had to be provided for otherwise. Thomas, being the second son, born on July 2, 1489, was, like his younger brother, destined for the Church, as were most youths who had no great expectations. They accepted their fate with neither enthusiasm nor disgust.

The two young men, as they came of good family, could not be expected to enter the priesthood in the haphazard fashion adopted by the majority of the clerics who, in the days before there were any ecclesiastical seminaries, learned just enough Latin to say Mass and wound up with the inadequate stipend of a chantry priest. Such a cleric would receive some rudimentary instruction from one of the rather uncouth parsons, of whom there were then, according to Sir Thomas More, far too many, and that was all. Instead of this, the young Cranmers decided to attend Cambridge University, such being virtually the only way for a cleric to obtain preferment. Of course the polish of a good education seemed desirable, apart from its being the road upward in the world.

Yet one should add of Thomas Cranmer that, so far from being unduly ambitious, he was not ambitious enough, quite content with his studies and then a fellowship, perhaps for the rest of his life, unless he obtained a small benefice and subsided into what Edward Gibbon was to call (speaking of eighteenth century parsons) "the fat slumbers of the Church." This unadventurous disposition was characteristic of him, a circumstance that makes his subsequent career a bit hard to explain.

In later life Cranmer used to tell of a cruel schoolmaster he had had, ascribing to the master's ill-usage his own constitutional timidity. Who this schoolmaster was we do not know, but he was probably a chantry priest, one of those employed to say Mass for the dead members of a local guild and eking out the pittance he received by taking in a few

6

pupils. Of these there were in all likelihood only a very few, for of the sons of the rustics living in or near Aslacton not one in twenty would have felt that he needed to learn how to read and write; and Aslacton did not have five hundred people in the hamlet. It is probable that the teacher had no more than very elementary knowledge to impart, and that he administered this merely by rote, quite unaware that the shy short-sighted Thomas was to become celebrated as a scholar, though his attainments here, even after his Cambridge years, did not make him first-rate according to the strict standards of scholarship. If the boy had shown, as may have been the case, that he had literary talents worth encouraging, a schoolmaster of this sort might have considered them of little, if any, value. Rough and boorish the man may have been, but all this also could have been exaggerated by Cranmer in later life.

Yet a "school" in our sense of the term should not be pictured, but rather a group of boys who found they could make their own lot easier by using young Cranmer as their butt, so diverting the attention of the schoolmaster from themselves. The man probably could teach what little he himself knew only by rule of thumb. Perhaps it was rather "by ferrule" for there were a great many teachers who simply lacked ability to recognize special aptitudes in their pupils or may even have resented such aptitudes and so have pounced upon the "odd" students for the slightest reason—unless Cranmer's short sight and diffidence were taken by a bullying schoolmaster as justification for being unkind. The whole story, as related in old age by Archbishop Cranmer to his secretary, may mean only that he was unduly sensitive, but it is clear that after fifty years the schoolmaster was still regarded with something like horror.

Here one is obliged to do some guessing, and to make deductions from general knowledge. We have all heard of schoolmasters, some of whom must be called adequately learned, who operated on the pedagogical principle that Latin grammar was absorbed by the backside rather than the brains, and who sometimes said as much—let us hope humorously. While a boy may sometimes have had his wits sharpened by fear, it also happened that a boy—especially one who was shrinking and refined—had his wits paralyzed by terror. I do not doubt that this schoolmaster accentuated his pupil's character, but I doubt very much whether he created it. And I am sure that, however little Thomas may have quaked at the clerical bully, however much he cringed at the brandished birch, he was too intelligent not to have learned something. One gathers that this process went on until the student, having absorbed all that this teacher had to impart, and no doubt having divined things which were not included in the formal lessons, was felt to be ready for the University. For that there had to be no graduation, in our sense of the term, because a system of "credits" was unknown. For Cranmer's first years there, Cambridge was to be no more than what we would consider a school. It may be that Mrs. Cranmer sent the boy there at the earliest possible moment to remove him—at least this may have helped her to make the decision—from that little country school where her son was so unhappy.

In all this there is some unavoidable guess-work. But with this we pass to more certain ground. The elder Cranmer died in 1501, and the smallness of his monastic bequests is surprising. Professor Pollard thinks it was because of the restraints imposed by making the Abbot of Welbeck overseer of the will and by then requiring the attestation of two other persons, Thomas Wilkinson (as that time Vicar of Whatton, and two years later himself the Abbot) and Edward Collinson, a canon of the Abbey. The reasoning is rather strange, as the reference to these Fathers rather obviously indicates a close and friendly relationship between them.

What is much more to the point is that the elder Cranmer did not have a great deal to leave, except for the estate, which was to pass to the eldest son. We may surmise that Cranmer had talked the matter over with his monkish friends, and had been given assurance that they were well enough off. It may have been at their suggestion that a few small clerical bequests went elsewhere. The chief of these was ten shillings for a new bell for the church at Whatton, where the father was buried. It can only be conjectural that the admission of his son to Welbeck Abbey had been so much as mooted, and it is quite certain that it would have caused resentment if, for any reason, there had been a refusal. When our Thomas Cranmer did go to Cambridge, it must have been a year or so after his father's death, and we may presume it was at the instance of his mother who, though she must have known that he felt no urgent call to the priesthood, also knew that a life of scholarly ease would be more to his taste than the stricter monastic obligations. Moreover, she was now free to use her own meager fortune for this purpose. Luckily she could find several colleges where the fees were almost nominal. The English universities still retained their medieval character and were not beyond the reach of people in very moderate circumstances.

We get a few other glimpses of Thomas Cranmer's boyhood in Aslacton. When Cranmer, as Archbishop, told Ralph

Morice something of those days, he did not confine himself
to memories of his schoolmaster, which fifty years later were
still rankling, but also said that his father saw to it—and
the account casts a pleasant light upon both father and son
—that the boy became proficient in the country sports then
in vogue, and this in spite of his being extremely short-
sighted, or "purblind," as Cranmer expressed it. He was in-
itiated into hunting and hawking and shooting with the
longbow and the crossbow. He acquitted himself fairly well,
and Morice testified how in his hours of leisure the elderly
man still enjoyed this form of diversion. But what struck
Morice most powerfully was how good a rider he was, even
in old age, never having the least fear of the wildest mount
in his stables; indeed, there was no horse that he could not
break. Morice marveled too at how an old man with such
poor eyesight could bring down his deer with his crossbow.
This was perhaps not so great a marvel as Morice supposed:
long experience and judgment in such matters made up for
defective sight. I find the picture most attractive; it makes
me regret that Thomas Cranmer could not have been the
Squire of Aslacton rather than the Archbishop of Canterbury. In that event we would have lost a great literary artist; the man himself would have been much happier.

This much should be added: there is not the slightest
indication that the young Thomas Cranmer had any literary
ambitions. Indeed, his mastery over words seems to have
been merely an accidental discovery made late in life, for
we never hear of his writing anything during his many years
at Cambridge. If it comes to that, he was unconscious of
his genius until the production of his exquisite Litany to-
ward the end of Henry VIII's reign. Then, of course, he
must have known and have been delighted, feeling, perhaps,

not only delight but some awe. Until his Litany he had been obliged, while in the royal service, to produce a good many official or semi-official reports, and no doubt he would have had to do much the same when he was a Cambridge Don, but he had never thought of these as having anything to do with literary art, so they were turned out hurriedly, merely with the intention of complying with inescapable duties, and are verbose, though they have the minor merit of conveying the writer's meaning.

The case is strange, in view of the present practice for writers to make their first efforts in adolescence or even childhood. It has almost come to be accepted as an axiom that unless one shows literary promise before he is twenty (and how many such writers wither and die while still a-borning!) he might as well give up all literary yearnings as hopeless. Even in Cranmer's day most writers began when they were rather young, as today it occasionally happens that a man turns out his first book when he is old. But in general the early sixteenth century was not particularly addicted to literature. Men knew, of course, that there had been a great literature in the classical past; some might perhaps have surmised that there would be a great literature again. But Cranmer lived in the trough of the wave, when most writing was considered merely utilitarian —most writing, but not quite all. Chaucer, who died a hundred years before Cranmer was born, had been a deliberate and careful artist, and he had put almost everything in his great line: "The lyf so short, the craft so long to lerne."

Would Cranmer have shared Chaucer's feeling? I doubt it very much. On the other hand I find it impossible to believe that he was not fully conscious of the greatness of what he had done in his Litany and the Book of Common

Prayer. Yet, before and after, he perpetrated a hundred times as much work which was pedestrian stuff quite unlike the finely chiseled and exquisite beauty of which we know he was capable. To me it is an impenetrable puzzle. The unsatisfactory solution I suggest is that he regarded ordinary writing—letters and reports and the verbose controversies—as one thing, and literary art as something in a completely different category. It was, moreover, an accident that made him the artist the world can never admire enough, just as it was an accident that dragged him out of his quiet room at Jesus College, Cambridge, and made him one of the main actors during one of the stormiest periods of English history.

What Cranmer entered Cambridge University to obtain —after getting his degree—was a quiet steady job which he seemingly was prepared to hold until death came for him. He may have entertained the possibility that, after he had obtained a fellowship at his college and then been ordained a priest (probably not until he had given the University many years of service—perhaps when he was in his forties or fifties), one of the clerical livings which were in the gift of his college would come his way. He would not have been averse to that, as it would have involved no radical change in his manner of life, but he was also content enough with things as they were. He was eminently the safe and sane man, whom one might be tempted to describe as a plodding mediocrity, had he not eventually proved that, whatever else he was, he was not that.

The university curriculum in those days was not much more than the learning of a scholastic method emptied of most of its former vitality, mere routine demonstration by formal syllogisms. People forgot that it had been quite otherwise in the true Middle Ages, which helps to explain the Reformation, for the very term implies a departure to a new and more vigorous mode of scholarship. However, not only those whom we describe as Protestants (a term not yet coined) but also the perfectly orthodox school of Humanists —men like More and Colet and their great friend Erasmus —were speaking with contempt of scholasticism, not guessing that it was destined to a new life. Yet Cranmer, after more than twenty years at Cambridge—first as a schoolboy, then as a university student proper, and finally as a fellow of his college—gives no indication that he found the kind of learning then in vogue unsatisfactory. He accepted the world as it was, and expected to do so to the end.

The young student—probably only about thirteen years old—enrolled first as a member of the small school conducted at Jesus College, Cambridge. During this period Latin was basic in everything, although he eventually proceeded to Greek and a little Hebrew and some knowledge of modern languages, his knowledge of the latter probably being filled out mainly while he was abroad in the King's service in his late thirties. As Jesus College did not specialize in Canon Law—the quickest way to ecclesiastical promotion—but in theology, it was mainly with theology that Cranmer came to concern himself, though his works suggest to me that his own reading was discursive rather than deep.

It would be wrong to say that no attention whatever was paid such subjects as the physical sciences or history, but it is true enough the attention was insufficient, unless a student was studying law or medicine. Even in the department of law the courses were limited in number, and they were still more limited in the way they were taught. The syllo-

13

gism was everything, and in those days it was Duns Scotus and not Thomas Aquinas who ruled the roost. A student had to be extremely intelligent to survive such a regimen. Indeed intelligence, or at least scholarship, was measured by the facility with which a student adapted himself to the kind of teaching then in vogue, and the tenacity of his memory.

The university methods had some severe critics. At Oxford about this time we had Thomas Linacre, who managed to combine an enthusiasm for Greek with a knowledge of medicine for which he was appointed royal physician. (Incidentally, he was the founder of the Royal College of Surgeons.) Also at Oxford was John Colet, a saintly man with a sharp tongue who, like Linacre, became a priest. At the same university Thomas More, the future Lord Chancellor, was plunging deep into his humanistic studies, until his father removed him fearing that his enthusiasm for Greek and anything else that had a literary tinge would hamper the law studies he intended his son to follow.

At Cambridge there was Erasmus, from 1511-14. Several years earlier he had perfected his Greek at Oxford, but in his Cambridge period he was primarily concerned with the Biblical criticism in which he was such a pioneer that his *Paraphrases,* appearing just before the outbreak of the storm in Germany, caused him to be accused of laying the egg that Luther had hatched. If Cranmer ever attended any of the lectures of Erasmus, he never mentions it in any of his writings.* One would not expect any personal encounter be-

* This may not mean much, however, since it was Erasmus' least attractive characteristic that he mentioned only those who might be of service to him—the nobly born and the wealthy. And also, Cranmer was reticent constitutionally.

tween the famous scholar and the young Don whom the former would have regarded as a nobody. But one is left with the impression that Cranmer was devoid of intellectual curiosity, especially regarding Biblical criticism. He may even have been a bit nervous at the possibility that someone would mention having seen him at a lecture by Erasmus, for the latter was already being spoken of in more conservative circles as inclined to dangerous novelties, to wild and unseemly jests, perhaps even to heretical notions. That was quite enough to keep Cranmer away.

No definite pronouncement can be made upon what is, in any event, a minor point, and an argument based on silence is notoriously unsafe. But it fits in with all we know of young Cranmer to think it more than likely that he did not wish to get mixed up with questionable speculations. He would have preferred keeping to the plain, safe road to his objective. The time of his awakening did come, though who succeeded in stirring him up we do not know. Indeed, it seems to have happened in spite of himself, by almost imperceptible degrees. It is fairly reasonable to believe that if Cranmer read Erasmus at all during those years, it was almost furtively. What Cranmer thought about him, if he thought about him at all, he kept to himself. For many years to come he confined himself to approved authors, lest he imperil his own situation.

Chapter Two

The Obscure Cambridge Don

It would be unsafe to say positively that Cranmer went to study at Cambridge University with the intention of eventually becoming a priest, though everything points to this as at least highly probable. The fellow of a college often remained in minor orders until, quite late in life, he received priesthood as a prerequisite to an ecclesiastical benefice. But a man with so little taste for adventure as this may have preferred the life with which he was already familiar rather than accept an appointment that might entail burdensome responsibilities. One does not picture the life of a country parson as very exciting, but Cranmer was the kind of a man who might be disturbed even at that thought.

Jesus College, which he entered about 1503, was a quiet little backwater, and to Thomas Cranmer may have been all the more attractive on that very account than one of the larger institutions whose standards and regulations were more exacting. It had been founded not long before by Bishop Alcock of Ely, Master of the Rolls under Henry VII. One glimpse we get of the Bishop suggests that he was a kindly man, for we hear that he once expostulated to the King when he found him giving a good thrashing to his son, Prince Henry. To this the irate father answered, "Never

entreat for him; this child will be the undoing of England!"
The remark need not be taken as prophetic; it is the kind
of thing that many a father has said. The truth is that the
King himself—and perhaps still more, the Lady Margaret—
should shoulder some blame on account of the strictness with
which they brought the boy up, a strictness from which the
Prince not unnaturally recoiled when he became King as
Henry VIII.

Bishop Alcock founded Jesus College by using the run-
down buildings and the endowments of a convent which,
as it was reduced to two nuns, was no longer serving any
very useful purpose. This suppression of moribund religious
houses every now and then occurred. For instance, St. John
Fisher, who became Chancellor of Cambridge University at
about the time Cranmer entered—before that he had been
the first Lady Margaret Professor of Divinity—did much the
same thing, as did Cardinal Wolsey, only on a larger and
more rapacious scale, when he was trying to obtain funds
for the grand college he projected at Oxford. Had Henry
VIII later been moderate in his expropriations no exception could have been taken, as it could have been said that
the suppression of decayed religious houses was for the benefit of the monastic system. Certainly no injury was inflicted
on the two Benedictine nuns who had lived in what was
made over into Jesus College, for they were merely wearing
a religious habit without any possibility of living like religious. They were therefore deposited in a well-managed
convent—with a sufficiency for their maintenance—and the
dilapidated buildings and their estates that had gone to rack
and ruin became Jesus College. It may have been unfortunate that Cranmer heard of this convent that had run to
seed, if that gave him a low opinion of convents in gen-

eral. However, this is not very likely. Such things happened now and then, and Cranmer could have heard of them without going to Jesus College.

If, as has been suggested, we have no indication that Cranmer showed any interest in the lectures given by Erasmus, we may presume that he did attend some of the lectures given by John Fisher. The latter was made Chancellor of the University in 1504, and as Lady Margaret Professor he spoke on Cranmer's own speciality of theology; moreover he enjoyed a great reputation for sanctity as well as learning. Surely the quiet stockily-built young Don would have gone now and then to hear *him*. The paths of Fisher and Cranmer were often to cross, but though Cranmer no doubt quite approved of the three treatises that Fisher wrote against Luther in the early twenties, and may even have considered Fisher in the right in supporting Queen Katharine during the trial conducted by Cardinals Campeggio and Wolsey, in the end—that was about five years later—the two men found themselves in opposed camps. Yet Cranmer apparently never lost his veneration for the man who laid down his life in support of Papal supremacy, though Cranmer (if his memory is to be trusted) began to pray for the abolition of that supremacy from about 1525.

What Cranmer said on the point is in all likelihood true. On every hand there were to be found men who denigrated the Papacy and in its stead exalted the Crown. This was not because they entertained non-Catholic doctrines such as Cranmer later himself held for some time—but because they lacked much zeal. But saints are rare at any time, and it is doubtful whether there could often have been less enthusiasm for sanctity than then. Even in the cloister religion was often a matter of routine, just as in the universi-

18

ties learning had degenerated into the application of lifeless formulas to matters that had slight bearing upon life. Cranmer may sometimes have thought that Jesus College, where he was a Don, was just about as moribund as the convent of St. Rhadegunde which it had replaced. If so, he was not noticeably distressed; that was the way the world was made.

The ills of the Church were evident, and a few people, such as John Colet—a most pious and orthodox man—spoke their minds plainly. People like Cranmer said nothing, having no ideas of special importance to contribute, being sluggish in mind and always afraid of coming into conflict with those in authority. But it would not be just to regard him as compounded merely of such elements. He, like all well instructed people, recognized that there was the need for some kind of reformation, but had little idea how it was to be brought about. Only this much may be said: after a long experience of worldly (and sometimes vicious) Popes, after a schism in Christendom, during which there had been two rival Popes (and once three), and the Captivity at Avignon, the prestige of the Papacy had been badly damaged. Obviously it was the Pope who should lead Christendom out of the morass into which it had stumbled, but few any longer looked for much help from that quarter.

Besides, the Pope lived far away and was reached with difficulty, and as likely as not, he would be badly informed of conditions prevailing in this country or that. It was coming to be believed that a strong King, ruling his own compact country, with many forces at his instant command, would be a better guardian of the Faith than it was possible for a Pope to be. In short, it was the determination of the English to be Catholic—and no other people in Europe were more free from heresy than themselves—that tended to augment the authority of the Crown in ecclesiastical affairs.

Though there were very few heretics in England—they were loosely called "Lollards," but few of them knew precisely what Wycliffe's doctrines had been or had so much as heard of the man—there were at least enough of them to be a vexation to Henry VIII. When at last he produced a polemical work—for he was somewhat vain of his theological powers, and these if not great were by no means negligible—he addressed it in confutation of Martin Luther. But there are reasons for believing that Henry had begun the composition of that book before the beginning of events in Germany. It was originally designed to correct English "Lollards," but switched to the castigation of Luther, who was creating much more of a stir in the world than a handful of English eccentrics had ever done.

In all this Henry VIII should be given credit for a sincere wish to prove his own orthodoxy and reclaim the erring, but he also wanted to obtain from the Pope some title such as the kings of France and Spain were able to flaunt. One need not blame him for trying to kill two birds with one stone, but it is questionable whether he would have gone to the trouble of producing a theological treatise * had he not had in mind the obtaining of a Papal honorific.

The existence of heresy was seldom to be encountered in

---

* Some professed to be astonished that Henry VIII could have written such a book and suggested that Sir Thomas More had been his "ghost." But More said most explicitly that he had had nothing to do with the book, except as a "sorter out" of its material. This has been sometimes taken to mean that More prepared the index—which, if the case, shows that More put himself to little trouble, the index being so poor. It seems to me more likely that More "edited" and arranged the King's manuscript to some extent.

England, though undoubtedly the Lutheran storm had repercussions there. More serious was the fact that there were many things of another sort amiss among the clergy, and that these had a rather bad effect upon the laity. Only occasionally could definite immorality be found among the clergy, and Sir Thomas More—who was in as good a position to know as anybody—soon after this affirmed in the most emphatic way that the priests in England compared very favorably with those in other countries. In remote parts of the country and, according to More, especially in Wales, some clerical concubinage was to be found. This kind of concubinage usually meant no more than that a priest lived with a woman in the state called "uncanonical marriage." Cardinal Wolsey himself had once had this kind of "wife," a Miss Larke, by whom we know that he had a son and a daughter. The situation carried with it no great odium, though it was regarded of course as highly improper. Henry VIII issued a proclamation against it, but without much effect.

When the monasteries and convents were suppressed during the years 1536-39 it was often charged by the visitators Thomas Cromwell sent out that they were hot-beds of vice, and if nothing could be proved, then there were broad insinuations of unnatural practices. Now Cranmer, familiar as he was with Welbeck Abbey, must have been well aware that these charges only exceedingly rarely had any foundation; but, of course, like everybody else, he must have known that "uncanonical marriage" sometimes existed, and in the University he probably heard rumors that some of the clerical Dons, who lived the lives of monks in their colleges, without, however, having monastic obligations, were not always strictly chaste.

The Papacy cannot be held responsible for this state of affairs, except perhaps as some high ecclesiastical personages gave a bad example. But though the English clergy—even if not to be held up as models—were far from being "corrupt," many people were inclined to think that clerical celibacy was too onerous an obligation, human nature being what it is; and this may serve partly to explain the episode of Cranmer's first marriage, though it should be repeated that he was not at that time a priest. In any event this was not a main issue in England. In that country, as throughout Christendom, it was evident that the vast majority of priests could endure the burden without too much bother.

Nor can the Papacy be very seriously blamed for the clerical exactions which by this time the English people—indeed, the people of most countries—commonly detested. While it may be true that the arrogance of some powerful people in Rome was obnoxious, the actual amount of money sluiced away by the Holy See was almost negligible. The fees demanded from a new bishop were large, but such fees only now and then became due, and in any case fell on the new bishop and not his flock. There was the annual payment of Peter's Pence, but this again was not a crushing sum. However, the local ecclesiastical officials felt, not altogether unreasonably, that they had to find some means of reimbursing themselves locally. And even when not a shilling was paid to the Holy See, it is to be feared that the clergy devised means of extracting money from the people. The perquisites of their office were not very lucrative and were often trifling, but charges were not the less irritating on that account. Wills were probated by the Church and not the secular courts—always with a scale of fees involved. But such fees did not begin to equal the death-duties that have to be paid to a modern state. The whole system of ecclesiastical taxation, though resented, was relatively light.

In all this the fact was lost sight of that the Church did a great deal for the material benefit of the poorer classes; that it maintained schools (in a rather haphazard way, perhaps, but usually gratis, or nearly so); and that in many places the wealthier monasteries made themselves responsible for the upkeep of roads and the repair of bridges and sea-walls where necessary. Yet the fees the Church demanded were all the more galling because the King was expected to make no calls upon his people except in a public emergency, such as a war. Normally the English people looked to the King to maintain all the ordinary functions of government out of his own very large endowments. Except for a few excise duties, the Crown had no other sources of revenue. All of which naturally and inevitably made people mutter about what they had to pay on certain occasions to their "rapacious clergy." These complaints did much to prepare for the coming upheaval.

Although during his Cambridge days Cranmer was not a part of the ecclesiastical machine—not even after his belated ordination as a priest—he undoubtedly heard much discussion of such matters, and as his was a receptive rather than a formative mind, he accepted what he heard. Even so, he prudently kept his mouth shut.

I do not intend to suggest that this accounts for Cranmer's case, but to provide a background for a surprising episode. When it occurred, Cranmer himself, though a Fellow of Jesus College, had not yet become a priest, but was bound only by the college regulations which demanded that the Fellows remain unmarried, though it is not impossible that some of them (or the Fellows of other colleges) had surreptitious extramural adventures. Thus it must be said that when he—suddenly and most surprisingly in one so circumspect—married, he broke no priestly vows, though it did inevitably mean that he was dismissed from his post.

In what follows it is probable that, though Cranmer acted very foolishly, in breaking a strict college rule, he may have been high-minded and even idealistic, though this does not alter the fact that his colleagues thought his conduct rather strange. They liked him personally, but the regulations had to be enforced; so out he had to go.

That he was well liked we can be sure from what will be related in the next chapter. That he had some small reputation as a scholar seems more than likely. And that his powers of expression made him a good teacher may be taken for granted. But he was cautious and conventional, partly because of his natural make-up and also because the age was not one in which intellectual daring conferred a great reputation. Moreover, when the exposition of novelties lifts a man above his fellows, those novelties have to be advanced with a force and pungency that Cranmer lacked —that is, if these novelties are to be rated as more than eccentricities. The young Don was not that sort of a man; moreover, he was, until late in his career at Cambridge, without the doctorate that would have conferred authority. It hardly became him to thrust himself forward, even had he wished to do so.

Cranmer was naturally modest and unassertive. Even in the classroom one imagines the short-sighted, stocky, rather undersized young man as being, if not precisely deferential, then at least as deferential as a teacher could be while yet imparting his knowledge. This, plus the fact that his reading was wide and always at his command,* brought him respect from Fellows and students alike, without arousing any special enthusiasm. That was no doubt just as well, at least as far as the college authorities were concerned, for it created no envy. And it is safe to say that he kept aloof from the little eddies of college politics that are everywhere to be found.

His private opinion about the importance of the authority of the King, as against that of the Pope, even in ecclesiastical concerns, was such as a professor would be careful not to vent before his students; and even to the Fellows in the college common-room he would give no more than a guarded assent to what the more daring said. It was still dangerous to speak one's mind too openly, for even during his later years in Cambridge, when some may have expressed sympathy with the New Learning, there were always scholars stubborn in the Old Learning who might exaggerate what was said. After all, the King himself had recently published a book † in which he had gone further than a good many people would have done in defense of the Supremacy of the Pope which, officially, remained unshaken in England. It was not for Cranmer, a Cambridge Don of no special standing, to rush ahead with ideas which, while he may have held

* This is at all events true of Cranmer in his later years. But it could hardly be true then unless he had acquired studious habits early.

† Henry's *Defence of the Seven Sacraments* seems mild in this respect to a modern Catholic. But we know that Sir Thomas More suggested that he tone this down, and that the King refused, urging that he was very much indebted to the Pope and giving a "secret reason" which More never divulged. One can only guess that it had something to do with the Papal dispensation that Henry might marry Katharine of Aragon, technically his sister-in-law. The King's book appeared in 1521, long before the appearance upon the scene of Anne Boleyn.

25

them privately, were to be aired with the utmost caution.

Cranmer was making no great mark at Cambridge, whatever small reputation he may have enjoyed there. He was quite content to tread well-beaten paths. In this way he could avoid all risk of getting into trouble; besides he did not feel as strongly about such things as did rasher and more hot-headed men. It was not so much a part of policy as of temperament. Without building up immense popularity, but by being instead courteous and unassuming, he was, without design, following the best possible method. Quite unwittingly, he was preparing himself for the illustrious career that never figured in his wildest dreams.

Chapter Three

Cranmer's First Marriage

Broadly speaking, in no country in Europe had the Church's discipline about the celibacy of the clergy been perfectly observed. If it comes to that, even in these days, when it is vastly better carried out, lapses occasionally occur, due to human frailty. The situation then was somewhat different: for centuries priests had been in many instances married men—as were some of the Apostles themselves—and celibacy was imposed only gradually and with difficulty. It was of course known to everybody that this was not part of the law of God, but an ecclesiastical regulation.

Yet for a long time it had been taken for granted, and though there might be a few who, in strictest privacy, questioned its advisability, the small handful of priests who in practice did not carry out their obligations were the ones least likely to express open disagreement. Yet Henry VIII was aware that there were some such people, and though he might wink at Wolsey's "uncanonical marriage," he issued a proclamation on the subject in general. Even so, we know that when Mary Tudor sent Dr. Taylor to the stake in 1556—for proven heresy and not on this account—it turned out that he had been married for twenty years and had a large family of children. But Taylor's marriage—for he tried to make it that and not merely concubinage, though it could not of course be open—had been made before witnesses. Doubtless there were other similar cases, but exceedingly few; more common, but still rare, were the cases of clandestine concubinage. It would have gone hard in Henry's time with anybody who openly announced his intention of flouting that particular point of Catholic practice.

In Cranmer's case, it must be said again that when he first married he was not a priest at all, though everybody (including himself) assumed that it was his intention to become one eventually. If he delayed about this, so did others, including the saintly Reginald Pole who, though he was elevated to the cardinalate in 1537, and in 1549 came close to being elected Pope, did not become a priest until early in 1556. So Cranmer's delay was not particularly unusual.

There may have been some who kept out of the priesthood because of motives less lofty than Pole's. Most of these, however, have something to be said for them; they had more scruples about breaking priestly vows than about ordinary fornication. This is not to suggest that this was the case with Cranmer. *He* was perfectly free to marry; all that we can say is that with him marriage ruined his career, or would have done so except for quite unforeseen circumstances.

He well understood that no Fellow of any college could bring a wife to live with him there, or even take a small house and still hold his position. Such a thing never happened until the reign of Edward VI, when the German theologian Martin Bucer was appointed to an Oxford professorship and openly introduced his wife into the college to which he was attached.* But by then things were vastly

* The poor woman—about whom we know very little except that she was large and was derisively known by a nickname which in Americanese would be "fatso"—died during his professorship, her husband quickly seeking refuge abroad when Queen Mary came to the throne in 1553. It is not pleasant to record that Mrs. Bucer's body was disinterred and—because there was no evidence to convict her of

different. Cranmer was well aware what would happen to *him,* if he married.

The town of Cambridge contained a number of ale-houses, but only two of these need be mentioned. One was the White Horse tavern, where the more daring spirits of the University used to forgather after 1521 to discuss what was amiss in the Church, among them the Robert Barnes, the Prior of the Augustinians, whom Henry VIII sent to the stake in 1540 as a heretic. Tyndale, Coverdale, Latimer, Bilney, Crome and Lambert (most of whom eventually suffered as martyrs) were also members of the group. For these men there was a back door by which they might come and go unobserved, and though they probably were not as yet avowed heretics, their Lutheran tendencies gave the tavern the name of "Little Germany." Cranmer, however, destined to be the most famous martyr of them all, kept away; it was all part of his character of caution.

The inn that he frequented was the Dolphin on Bridge Street, a site where Trinity College now stands. It was near Jesus College and the Fellows could meet other members of the University there. Professor Pollard represents this place as a kind of hotel, but it was probably only a pub, though no doubt overnight guests could be accommodated there. Pollard makes much of the fact that Thomas Cromwell's father kept a tavern (as did William Cecil's), a point which was beside the mark, for it was a detriment rather than an advantage to the son. Even if the landlord of the Dolphin had been a fairly prosperous person, he could have had no social standing, and it seems quite absurd for Foxe to describe the Dolphin's barmaid, Black Joan, as a gentleman's

heresy, in which case her body would have been burned—thrown out on a dunghill.

daughter. Her very name suggests that she was treated with off-hand familiarity by those who went there, though this does not mean that she was not a good girl, or that she was like the one in Masefield's *Everlasting Mercy:*

> *"Fifteen arms went round her waist;*
> *And then men ask, "Are barmaids chaste?"*

The present Poet Laureate is a doubtful authority, for though he did work for a short time in his youth in Luke O'Connor's bar in New York City, he assuredly saw no barmaids there. Black Joan may have been a relation of the landlord's; if so she was still not a "gentleman's daughter," and the fact that she was doing this sort of work indicates that she was much below Cranmer in social rank, even if, as the son of the Squire of Aslacton and the Fellow of a college, he was, himself, hardly of exalted station. If she was anything like the barmaids I have known in England, she was buxom and given to free exchanges of not very refined badinage with the customers, but again I say this does not necessarily mean that she was like Mr. Masefield's barmaid. Yet one suspects that in the company of the lively young woman Mr. Cranmer may sometimes have relaxed more than was usual with him, and that Black Joan saw to the rest.

It must not be stated as a fact that there was a pregnancy before marriage, but if this did happen, there was nothing in those days corresponding to a "shotgun" wedding. Such an incident was common enough, and nothing much could be done about it, nor did people even try to do much. If Cranmer came to the girl's rescue he must have acted of his own volition, and nobly. In any event the marriage was most rash: it meant dismissal from his Fellowship, and it is hard to see what kind of job would be open to him, unless that of an usher in a small school or a lawyer's clerk, both so miserably paid that he could have hardly supported a wife and child upon the pittance he would receive. Yet marry Black Joan is just what Cranmer did.

Perhaps he hoped that somehow—the "somehow" of a man at his wits' end—he could keep his marriage secret. Since there is no record of a marriage ceremony, in all likelihood the marriage was one of the "precontract" variety, valid enough but consisting merely of privately given vows. However it was, Black Joan's condition must soon have been all too evident to those who went to the Dolphin, and they may have suspected that the straight-laced Mr. Cranmer was the father. That could have been thought most amusing.

Had Thomas Cranmer been a scamp he could have laughed the matter off and allowed people to suppose that this was a mere liaison. That might have made him (and Black Joan) the butt of some coarse jests, and perhaps a wigging in private from the Master of his college, but it would have left his Fellowship safe. Or he might have tried to get the girl sent somewhere else, to bear their child where she and he were not known. If these shabby expedients came to his mind, perhaps he saw that they would not work; he made a clean breast of things and took his medicine.* From that day he ceased to be a Fellow of his college.

Judging from what subsequently happened the Master of Jesus College and the other Fellows did not hold Cranmer's

* One is obliged to conjecture, but we must presume there was no ordinary marriage before a priest. For that, there would be a calling of the banns and similar publicity. Yet all this may have occurred, and the child conceived after marriage. As there is no record of any marriage before a priest, it is more likely that the thing happened as has been suggested.

31

conduct seriously against him. Though under the college regulations he had to leave, they were sorry that he had to depart. It is quite possible that some of his associates had had their little adventures, and that if in any of their cases a pregnancy had resulted, they would not have behaved as honorably as Thomas Cranmer. If a Fellow who was a priest had been involved in such a predicament, he might have been permitted to remain, for his priesthood would have invalidated marriage. But Cranmer was not a priest, and he admitted the marriage. Perhaps with some wondering respect at his scruples, they had no choice but to call for his resignation.

There are men of our own time—not many of them, to be sure, but there are a few—who feel that if they have had relations with a woman they are obligated to her, whether or not there is a pregnancy. Needless to say fornication in itself does not create any bond, unless a pledge of marriage has been given, and only too often such pledges have been repudiated. It must be added that, at that time, a private vow was held to be marriage, of a sort.* In later years we shall find Cranmer trying to establish that Anne Boleyn had a precontract before she married Henry VIII, and that he tried to do the same in the case of Katherine Howard and one of the lovers she had had as a girl. Katherine probably lied, admitting no more than the guilty relationship. Young Cranmer was above-board. If he had given in to a momentary weakness, it would have been understandable. Upon the

---

* I do not know how it is at present under Scots law, but it will be remembered that Robert Burns in the eighteenth century claimed that Jean Armour, who had borne him a child, was his wife by private promise. Burns and Jean had to sit on the stool of repentance in the kirk for their misdemeanor, but they were successful in the end against the girl's father, who objected to the poet.

whole he had behaved admirably afterwards. It should be understood that if I am correct in the suppositions that force themselves upon my mind, while I do not approve of the weakness, I admire his honesty. He had behaved as well as was possible under the circumstances.

But now what was the ex-Don to do for a livelihood? When he was an Archbishop rumors kept cropping up that he had at one time been an ostler. Strictly speaking, they were malicious untruths; yet they may have had just a grain of truth in them. Unless he was going to return home and abandon Black Joan just when she needed him most, it is not unlikely that Cranmer stayed with her at the Dolphin and that there such a good hand with horses would have lent a hand for a week or two with whatever needed to be done. But if this ostler story is true at all, it meant only that Cranmer stayed at the Dolphin while taking his bearings. In any event this period was very brief, for he obtained a position as special lecturer in theology at a small Benedictine college. The remuneration would have been meager but the work was somewhat along the same lines as the work he had previously done.

Luckily for him Black Joan died in childbirth and with her her baby, so his escapade was over. That the Master and Fellows at Jesus College did not consider Cranmer disgraced is amply proved by the fact that they promptly reelected him to his lost Fellowship. He had a modest reputation as a scholar; he was well liked by his former associates; he was not to be irretrievably ruined because of a single false step. And as they no doubt had often gone to the Dolphin in their time, they knew Black Joan—possibly things about her that the simple-minded Cranmer never discovered. At all events they were willing for Cranmer to return.

It is impossible to say what Cranmer's feelings were about his first wife. They could, of course, have been very deep and devoted, and he no doubt felt sorrow and was chastened by the whole episode. But whatever he may have felt at the time, it was naturally not a matter about which he ever talked much in later life. Upon reflection he must have seen that the escapade, or accident, was one that had turned out much better than he had any right to expect.

The treatment given him at Jesus College was kind and considerate and might not have been accorded another man. He was allowed to feel that he had emerged with no disgrace, but perhaps rather well. He picked up the thread of his studies and appeared—maybe a little crestfallen—before his students once more. After this, the authorities felt sure that Cranmer would never again repeat his ludicrous mistake but would be more careful than ever not to do anything odd. After a decent interval—when he was about thirty but just when we do not know—he was ordained a priest and a few years afterwards became a doctor of divinity, a degree which greatly increased his academic standing.

In all probability he would not have got much further at Cambridge. A Mastership was not something he could look for, even had he been the kind of man to push his own fortunes. In due course he might have obtained a comfortable little benefice, had that been what he wanted, but apparently the sedate, stocky little man was content to let matters follow their own course. Indications are that he had no thought except to go on with the quiet dull routine of Jesus College.

Chapter Four

The Unsought Chance

Cranmer had proved conclusively that he was indifferent to getting on in the world, even the small world of Cambridge University, if only by the startling imprudence of his marriage. Towards that marriage I trust due sympathy has been shown, and I certainly approve his unworldliness. But of course there were features of that case to which I do not give approval at all, even though I see that Cranmer behaved well in very difficult circumstances. Little as I like to see a man thinking continually of the main chance, I do not like seeing anybody act like a fool, and it had been exceedingly foolish for Cranmer to act in a way that would have ruined him except for the totally unexpected turn of events.

The Black Joan episode serves to show what kind of man he was, one capable, despite all his reserve and caution, of sometimes throwing even elementary prudence to the winds. It was a streak in his character which was to reappear, very seldom, to be sure, but which casts some light upon the kind of man beneath the apparently impeccable restraint that most of Cranmer's life seemed to demonstrate.

The glacially correct façade concealed rashness and human weakness; it also concealed fiery qualities which he guarded more carefully than ever for the rest of his days, except that there were to be at least two other occasions, many years later, when his rashness got the better of him.

His strange first marriage has been stressed for this reason; it serves to explain a Cranmer who was not all of one piece.

One characteristic, however, was constant, being ingrained in him: his lack of ambition. Similarly, when wealth came to him, he not merely said that it meant little or nothing to him, but he proved it by his comportment. The time, indeed, was past when a Wolsey—although Wolsey was not only Archbishop of York but also Papal Legate and Lord Chancellor—could amass an immense fortune. On the contrary, the period of Cranmer's prelacy was one in which Henry VIII—and later the nobles who acted for the boy King, Edward VI—took big bites in the endowments of the Church. Cranmer himself was to suffer, as when Henry VIII calmly appropriated Knoll, today the largest house in England with its 365 rooms, though nominally he was recompensed with some other property in exchange. Cranmer summed up the situation himself when he said, at the end of his life, that, though as Archbishop of Canterbury he owned many manors, he thought he was really worse off materially than he had been as a Fellow of Jesus College. One fancies that at the time of his great position in the world, there were moments when he regretted he had not been allowed to live out his days in obscure quietness at Cambridge University.

Such private grumblings to friends about his worsened material condition did not occur very often, and are not to be taken too seriously. They may even have had a touch of humor, though this quality was not among Cranmer's most strongly marked characteristics. Even during the reign of Edward VI, when many bishoprics were heavily despoiled by those in authority, his archdiocese went almost scot-free. And at that time—when he was making his complaints, such as they are—probably the greatest drain upon him was the hospitality he gave to theologians from abroad. He was glad to entertain them and derived much from their advice, but they and their wives and families sometimes had a way of staying with him for inordinately long periods. But it must be granted that he had little concern for his personal material interest, being far more troubled by the despoiling of others—some bishops and many of the parochial clergy, for whom he felt duty bound to make some protest—as well as for the robbery of schools and chantries and guilds. Being the kind of man he was, though, and in any case not being in a position to storm about such injustices, the disapproval he expressed was mild. About his personal possessions he was about as indifferent as such a man could be. All this was but another aspect of his almost total lack of ambition.

Whether or not Thomas Cranmer was like the man in the parable to whom the host said, "Friend, go up higher!" something like this happened to him, to a great extent against his own inclinations. The merest chance brought the obscure Cambridge Don to the notice of the King. Henry, taking a liking to him and seeing the uses to which he might be put, obliged him to play a part in the public eye that he had never so much as dreamed of.

It happened this way: after Cardinal Wolsey's fall at the end of 1529, the King—in spite of the personal animosity of Anne Boleyn and the social and personal animosity of many of the nobles—remained in a double mind. Sir Thomas More, Wolsey's successor as Chancellor, a very able and upright man admired by everybody, had accepted office only on condition that he would not be asked to do anything about Henry's divorce, of which the King knew well he disapproved. But even if More had had Wolsey's diplomatic finesse and lack of scruples, it is hard to see what he could have accomplished, and nobody else, as yet upon the scene, was doing anything. For a while Henry was so discouraged that he was almost ready to abandon the whole project. But shrill-voiced Anne, though not a very clever woman, was at least intelligent enough to know that this would mean an end to her ascendancy, or that she would be forced to become the King's mistress, accepting as reward something less than the Crown itself.

Henry could foresee trouble if he proposed to make Anne his queen, and so was half-inclined to bring the adroit Wolsey back from the archdiocese of York to get him what he wanted. It was because the Duke of Norfolk was all too well aware that this was likely to happen that he concocted a charge of treason against the Cardinal. The King allowed it to go through because he suspected that the charge was bogus, and because Wolsey, upon his return to London, might well be able to clear himself of all accusations, whereupon Henry would have an opportunity to utilize his services again.

Thomas Cromwell, formerly Wolsey's chief man of business, did not openly align himself with the Duke and still professed the greatest loyalty to his old master. He himself had not yet attained any very important position, though Henry now and then consulted the square-cut figure with the waddling walk and the swivel-eyes. Those eyes were carefully watching events, and Cromwell was by no means sure that Wolsey would not regain much of his old power—in which case it would be very dangerous for him to be known as one of Wolsey's enemies. He may already have thought out what was to be his subsequent mode of procedure, but he dared not bring this out openly so long as Wolsey might regain the King's favor; Cromwell was not able to do more than bide his time.

It so happened that, as early as 1527, two men had suggested to the King that the universities of Europe be asked to give their opinion on whether it was within the Pope's competence to issue a dispensation for a man to marry his brother's widow, always of course with the proviso that that marriage had been consummated, which Katharine of Aragon always asserted was not the case. One of these men was a Brigittine monk of Syon, but as Henry was still turning over other possibilities in his mind—especially that Wolsey might be able to unravel the tangle by the ordinary and more satisfactory means, these suggestions were not acted upon.

The idea was not a bad one, even though it did not help matters a great deal when tried later. It was not merely a question of Oxford and Cambridge, for if they gave an opinion in favor of the King it would naturally be supposed that they had done so under duress. Of course, it could also be taken for granted that the universities of Spain, or other territories under the Emperor Charles V, would not answer as free agents. But it was a different matter with the rest of the European universities; it was thought (and correctly) that the Pope would not interfere even with those in the Papal States, as this was an abstract question about which various views might legitimately be held.

More than that, Clement VII had more than once spoken in such a petulant way of a matter he found a great nuisance that there were reasons to believe that he would welcome a Henrician judgment on the part of the universities. This opinion could be represented as that of a "scattered

Council" of the Church and thus help to relieve the Pope of responsibility. Clement could say that in view of the majority opinion of this "Council" he should himself decide for Henry. This might also induce the Emperor to give up the fight he was making for his aunt, Katharine of Aragon. Who was he to stand out so stubbornly against all these learned men? With no loss of face he could back down.

There was, however, a good deal of unreality in the scheme, ingenious though it was, so that one can easily see how it emanated from the mind of a scholarly recluse out of touch with the world as it was. It might also be remarked that, until Mary came to the throne, Cranmer was forever toying with the idea of a Council—in later years, of a Council of Protestants. But this first notion of his seemed to be worth trying, though again we have an example of Cranmer's lack of originality. He was always a man who followed, not one who led. But he happened to bring the university scheme forward at the right moment, where his predecessors had been inopportune. Even so, nothing was done about it for several months.

So much for the idea in itself; the meeting between Cranmer and the King was quite fortuitous. Henry was addicted to moving from place to place, usually with the excuse of finding better hunting, sometimes to escape one of the frequent pestilences, but often, it would seem, only because of his restlessness. At any rate, on July 4, 1529—that is, before Cardinal Wolsey had fallen—we find the King at Waltham, from which place he went on the sixth to hunt at his manor at Hunsdon, going the next day to Tyttlehanger and three days later returning to Waltham. At Waltham was the famous abbey founded by Harold, the last of the Saxon Kings, though of course during the centuries it had been greatly enlarged. Still, some of those with Henry VIII had to be lodged elsewhere. That was how it came about that the royal Almoner, Dr. Fox, and Stephen Gardiner, who had been in the Cardinal's service but was now in the King's, were sent to a Mr. Cressy's house nearby.

Both Gardiner and Fox were Cambridge men and at Mr. Cressy's house they found another Cambridge man staying, Thomas Cranmer, of whose modest reputation for scholarship they were aware. These important men—both of them near to bishoprics—may have treated Cranmer with a tinge of patronage, as they knew that they were on the point of "arriving," whereas nobody expected Cranmer ever to amount to much. That he was at Mr. Cressy's was a further proof of this, if proof were needed, for he had gone there to earn a little extra money during vacation in the capacity of tutor to Cressy's sons. When the visitors heard that Cranmer and Cressy were related, one imagines there may have been a further arching of eyebrows; so even this trifling job was obtained for this reason!

But Thomas Cranmer was an old acquaintance and the talk at table naturally turned on the divorce from the Queen the King hoped to obtain from the Pope. It was in one of these sessions that Cranmer came out with his suggestion about canvassing the European universities. This may have been because Gardiner, about the same age as Cranmer and looking like him to some extent—having a thoroughly ecclesiastical face, but one in which the eyebrows seemed almost to meet—bluntly demanded his opinion. In this Gardiner could scarcely have expected to be presented with a plan of campaign by the self-effacing Don, but he was interested in knowing what Cranmer, as a theologian, thought.

41

The two visitors, though by no means ignorant of theology, had made canon law the field of their major studies.

The question was probably asked by way of making conversation, for Cranmer was not the man to thrust unsought views upon people. Moreover, his visitors had opportunity to consult the best theologians in the country. Still, as this was what everybody in England was talking about just then, Gardiner wanted to know what Cranmer thought. It was then that the Don who was for the moment tutoring Mr. Cressy's sons produced the plan of consulting the universities. He probably did not try to palm it off as his own bright idea—for he was modest—but he may have given some improvements to what had been proposed two years earlier. In any event this was accepted as Cranmer's suggestion and as such presented by Gardiner and Fox to the King.

Cranmer had the advantage of being able to outline the plan at leisure and before men he knew. And though he was inclined to be rather verbose, verbosity was one of the characteristics of the age. It was manifested even in the English works soon to be written by Sir Thomas More, though in him it was redeemed by his racy humor and his gift for telling amusing stories. Cranmer was no Thomas More, but in his Cambridge classroom he had developed a power of clear exposition. Gardiner and Fox were impressed with an idea that seemed plausible.

King Henry when told of what Cranmer had said—he too was often verbose, though there were times when, by sheer force of his powerful personality, he could be remarkably succinct—exclaimed, "That man has the right sow by the ear!" Yet Henry, as was customary with him, procrastinated. For the moment he did nothing, and Cranmer returned to Jesus College, to give his usual lectures—expecting to hear no more about the matter—when suddenly he was summoned to Greenwich to see the King.

Then Henry VIII asked—and to ask was to order—that the Boleyns give Dr. Cranmer hospitality as he was to put in writing, and in greater detail, the idea that he had advanced in conversation in the summer. This was soon done and then Henry started with the English universities. But as Pollard says, Cranmer had "no part in the maneuvers of the King's agents to obtain a favorable verdict." After all, he was still only an inconspicuous man who happened to be the Fellow of an inconspicuous college. As one without any influence or energetic drive he was useless for the royal purpose. There were a dozen men available who had proved their competence, whereas Cranmer, so far as anybody knew, had no competence at all. Such matters were put in the hands of those able to pull the necessary wires at home and abroad.

But that Cranmer had made the suggestion was held to his credit. And Henry and the Boleyns believed that he would be useful in other ways. He was rewarded with the archdeaconry of Taunton in Somerset, and by this means obtained a rather good income. He lived at the Boleyns' luxurious house and obviously was growing in the King's favor; but nobody guessed as yet to what eminence he would rise. It had all been due to that accidental meeting with Gardiner and Fox, to that and to Cranmer's own ingratiating manner. But though he might now be considered as a person in the royal service, it was not imagined—even by his patrons—that he would go much further. Again he was content with what he had.

Chapter Five

Ambassador and Archbishop

Whatever else may be said of Thomas Cranmer, he was one of those who acted on the principle *Nolo episcopari*. He was constitutionally a mild and inoffensive scholar, and though he served Henry VIII, he was not looking for honors, not even a bishopric, let alone an archbishopric. This may not have been merely because he felt himself unworthy —though a graceful and genuine modesty cannot be denied him—but rather because he tended to shrink from responsibility and because he preferred the quiet life of study and the use of the college library. However, he knew by now that Cambridge University was a thing of the past, for there was no resisting the overbearing will of a King like Henry. Cranmer was doing what he was told because he had no choice in the matter. He could only hope that after he had performed his mission he would be permitted to retire to some relatively obscure benefice.

Though Henry and the Boleyns had already decided that he was, in his way, an exceptional man, his character remains a good deal of a puzzle. Equally mistaken are those who consider him devious, or nothing but a sycophant, or very simple. The latter have this to be said for them: his affability and willingness to help gave people the impression that he was naïve, and people who were not at all naïve —such as the King and Thomas Cromwell who had by now begun his calculated ascent to power—believed that his apparent naïveté (one of the elements from which he was compounded) might be a cloak behind which they could operate. But that he was not self-seeking can be demonstrated from things that will be narrated below.

Thomas Boleyn was a man who had made a fortune as a mercer, one of the few trades in England where this was possible, and at that time by far the most remunerative trade of all. He had grown rich enough to have married one of the Howards, a great match for a man like him. Probably it was at least partly due to this connection that he had also obtained official employment—as joint-Constable of Norwich castle, then on brief embassies to France and Spain, and again as Treasurer of the King's household. Still more it may have been due to his complaisance about his daughter Mary's becoming the King's mistress. He was duly rewarded, first by being created Viscount Rochford and then Earl of Wiltshire. But as Henry was not accustomed to entrust official missions to men who had no ability, we must suppose that Boleyn was not deficient, though he is not recorded to have said anything very memorable, and though the contemporary painting of him depicts a swarthy, quite undistinguished little man, with hair plastered down, sleek and sly.

When his other daughter Anne arrived from France and attracted the King's attention—which became a furious desire to possess her as he had previously possessed Mary— Boleyn supposed at first, as did most people, that she had become Henry's mistress, and it caused him no shock. She denied this to him, and her denial happened to be true, for despite Henry's greasily importunate love letters Anne held him off, her settled determination being that she should become Queen by ousting Katharine of Aragon, a circumstance which helped in Boleyn's further advancement. What also helped was that when in 1536 Henry beheaded Anne and her brother (by that time Viscount Rochford) their father never lifted a hand to help them. By whatever ignoble means, he was resolved to get on in the world—and so he did, after a fashion.

Cranmer himself professed to find the Boleyns edifying, especially of course Anne, who was probably the best of a bad bunch. Chapuys, the clever Savoyard whom the Emperor sent to England as his Ambassador, and who remained there until the time of Katherine Parr, Henry's sixth and last wife, described them in one of his letters to Charles V as "more Lutheran than Luther himself," which they were not, except in the sense that they were all for Henry's abrogating the jurisdiction of the Pope. The phrase might be more accurately turned upon Henry, as being more Catholic than the Pope. The Boleyns were in fact only faintly interested in religion but were quick to use the turmoils of the age to their own advantage.

Anne who was the central figure of the group was not without some piety, if we may judge from her wishing to have the Blessed Sacrament in an oratory adjoining the room in the Tower in which in 1536 she was awaiting execution, but she can hardly be credited with Henry's devoutness, which may seem of a queer sort but which was evidently quite genuine and also constant. Cranmer, too, as became a parson, was pious, or at least had the habit of striking pious attitudes and using pious expressions. How much he had hid his heart in heaven may be open to question, and one gathers that when he frequently used the expression "the Gospel," he did not attach to it the meaning that we do. It would seem that the Gospel meant merely a heavy emphasis on one or two texts, such as "Render to Caesar the things that be Caesar's," along with St. Paul's admonition to be subject to the powers that be. Subservience to the monarch was, if not the whole duty of the Christian life, one of the main parts of it. The doctrine of the divine right of kings was not first propounded by James I; although not so definitely formulated in Henry VIII's time, it was there, and had been developing earlier. If this was not "the Gospel," as the term went, it is impossible to get any clear idea what was meant. Lutheranism, or anything that we now would regard as Protestantism, was not implied. All these people—lax though the majority of them were, just as a few were fervent—were Catholic in belief. As yet all of them admitted the supremacy of the Pope.

Cranmer is sometimes described as the Boleyns' chaplain, and even as Anne's tutor. While it is likely enough that he, as a university Don, gave some instruction occasionally to Anne—who was without much education—and said Mass now and then in the Boleyns' chapel, he did not serve in either capacity regularly or by formal appointment. He was living in their grand London house merely because Henry VIII had a way of quartering people with this or that family, as his palaces were usually overcrowded. By going to live with them while he prepared his brief for the King Cranmer ingratiated himself with them and became, as it were, a member of their family as well as of their entourage.

Thus it came about that when old Boleyn went abroad

47

in 1530 on a diplomatic mission to the Emperor, it was decided that Thomas Cranmer should go along. He had no carefully defined position with the group, but there were several ways in which he might be serviceable; and he was an agreeable person to have in one's train. The little pig-like eyes of Henry were good at picking out people who might be of use, and while Boleyn and his party were abroad Thomas Cromwell rose to the fore with several ingenious suggestions, one of which was going to bring a complete change to Cranmer's fortunes.

Though the main matter was to see the Emperor and get him to see reason regarding his aunt, Katharine of Aragon, the possibilities of Cranmer's plans about gathering the opinions of foreign universities were also to be explored, and it was thought advisable to have the concocter of that plan on hand for consultation. As Cranmer had foretold, the Pope—at least at first—raised no difficulties about discussions on an abstract point, concerning which more than one view was permissible. But Henry (or his agents) made the mistake of trying to bribe the university faculties, and even paid indigent rabbis for their opinions. Naturally this discredited the affair when news of it reached Rome, so that Clement forbade any university professors to sit in judgment on the case, later making his prohibition apply only to those who, by taking money, had to be considered suborned. But as bribery was not easy to prove, the buying of favorable opinions went on. Even so, Henry could obtain only a doubtful bare majority. Cranmer, as a man unaccustomed to practical affairs, took little if any part in a performance which, as he was a university professor himself, would (let us believe) have disgusted him. The dirty work was entrusted to others. Even Reginald Pole consented to present Henry's case to the Sorbonne, but he did not himself argue in favor of it or press the issue, and his hands gave out no English gold. This was hardly necessary in France, where its King, Francis I, was known to be backing Henry.

The question was debatable on the basis of Old Testament texts, but it was nevertheless confusing. In Leviticus there was a passage that declared a man's marriage to his brother's widow impermissible—or, at least, it could be taken in that sense—whereas in Deuteronomy there was another passage that laid on a man the obligation of marrying her, so as to "raise up seed" to the dead man. The confusion was made worse by the fact that we read how Christ, when presented with this very case, swept it aside as a sophistry of the Sadducees and would give no answer except that in heaven there was no taking in marriage or giving in marriage. About such matters Cranmer, as a theologian, may have been asked to advise the canon lawyers in the party, but about that we have no information.

We do know of certain events that occurred at Nuremberg, where the embassage caught up with Charles V. It was certainly an extraordinary lapse in tact (or even plain common sense) to have sent Boleyn to the Emperor in a cause where his personal interests were involved. When the Earl of Wiltshire told Charles that he was empowered to offer the return of Katharine of Aragon's dowry, plus a handsome addition, the sleek old man, who had believed this would get the Emperor to drop his opposition to his aunt's divorce, only drew Charles' wrathful answer that his aunt was not for sale. Charles was, indeed, so incensed by such a proposition that he told Boleyn flatly he would not listen to another word from him, but that somebody else

49

would have to do the talking. It was the most peremptory thing that could have been said to an accredited Ambassador.

At Nuremberg Cranmer, having plenty of time on his hands, became acquainted with a man who passed under the name of Osiander, which was not his real name but a pseudo-Greek form into which he had contrived to transmogrify Hosmer. He was not precisely a Lutheran—for many shades of opinion had already begun to appear in Germany —but was at least close to being one. Though he was a priest, we do not hear of his having married, which was about the first step a Lutheran took, almost *de rigueur*, for sometimes even Abbots who had associated themselves with the Reform introduced wives into their monasteries. What matters is that Osiander had a niece acting as his house-keeper and that Cranmer had already shown himself susceptible to women. The girl, for her part, seems to have been equally susceptible to men, for she married three times. Now she was attracted by the visiting English priest, who must have been at least twenty years older than herself. Her uncle told her that this looked like a coming man, or she may have divined as much herself.

We lack many of the details of the situation, but she set out to win him, aware of course that under canon law a priest is incapable of valid marriage but not bothering herself much with such considerations. This Margaret does not seem to have had much difficulty in drawing Cranmer into her toils, but under the circumstances the marriage must have been irregular in character (as well as invalid), for any member of the entourage of the English Ambassador must have been a marked man, concerning whom somebody (perhaps the Emperor himself) would have been prompt to in-form Henry VIII. However, nothing leaked out about it—not then.

Dr. Cranmer was not permitted to enjoy the society of the buxom Margaret for long, as the Emperor was going into Italy to be crowned there by the Pope, and the train of Englishmen had to go where he went. Clement's attitude was that the question of the validity of the marriage of Henry VIII and Katharine of Aragon was still an open one. At any rate he had made no definite decision but was doing his best to maintain friendly relations with all the crowned heads concerned—Henry himself, Charles V and Francis I. He also was of the opinion that if Anne Boleyn was not already Henry VIII's mistress, she would become that before long, and then, he believed, the King would soon grow tired of her. And though he had forbidden any court to hand down a judgment on a matter which had been appealed to the Holy See, he would have been relieved had the Archbishop of Canterbury (William Warham) granted an annulment, and the Holy See was then prepared to recognise a *fait accompli*. This, however, Warham, despite dire threats now being made by Cromwell, refused to do.

Cranmer, while in Rome, offered to debate the matter with anybody willing to accept his challenge. But as the terms of the debate were of his divising and presumed too much, nobody came forward. However, Cranmer, far from being aggressive, was so courteous and deferential that he made a good impression on everybody, including the Pope. Clement VII might not have felt as he did had he known about Mrs. Cranmer in Nuremberg, but as he was in total ignorance about her, and as it soon came out that Cranmer was not one of Luther's adherents, the Pope gave him the title of Penitentiary for England. This of course showed good-will towards Cranmer personally but perhaps was primarily intended to placate the King of England.

Henry VIII, for his part, was busy all this time in "cultivating" the Papal Nuncio, Baron del Burgo, carrying matters so far with that famous geniality of his that many came to suspect there was some kind of secret understanding between King and Pope. He actually, upon opening Parliament—and the Parliament through which he intended to push his final breach with the Holy See—had the Baron sit at his right hand on the dais. The news of that naturally traveled back quickly to Rome and gave, as it was intended to give, a false impression, and so threw the Pope off his guard. The bluff Henry was an exceedingly artful person, whereas of Cranmer it must be said that though he was not nearly so simple as many people supposed, he was not addicted to deceit, even if occasionally he allowed some coloring of it to appear when obliged to obey a command that he could not refuse. His was rather a faculty for getting into scrapes.

He found himself in one now, on account of his marriage (if one can really call it that) to Osiander's niece. For a courier arrived with a letter that ordered him to return to England, and he learned that he was to be appointed Archbishop of Canterbury. Now Margaret in Nuremberg was really going to be a complication, for while Henry had tolerated Wolsey's relations with Miss Larke, he would be sure to feel very differently about a new man being brought in as Primate (and bound to receive criticism for being put over the heads of men whom most people would consider better qualified for the position than himself). If Cranmer had had any inkling of what was to happen he would have

certainly found means of holding Margaret off. Now what
a predicament he was in: at once a married man and the
man selected to be Archbishop of Canterbury!

What had happened was that William Warham, the aged
Archbishop of Canterbury, had died the previous August
24th. That he was allowed to die in bed possibly saved him
from a very different fate, for Anne Boleyn, hearing that
her father had been able to accomplish nothing with the
Pope or Emperor had grown very impatient, and when Warham refused to hear the King's cause in face of the general
prohibition issued by Clement VII, Cromwell had begun to
talk of issuing a *Praemunire* against him and of hanging
him on a gallows as high as that used for Haman—which,
it may be remembered, towered up fifty cubits. The bit
about such a gallows was of course a rhetorical flourish,
mere bluster, but there is no doubt that Warham would
have gone to the block had he not been ill and over eighty.
As he was sure to die before long, Henry would be free to
select another Archbishop of Canterbury.

There were other men in England who had a vastly better claim to the Archbishopric—Tunstall of Durham, for instance, or Gardiner of Winchester. But Tunstall could be
left out of consideration, ostensibly on account of his age,
but really because he was known to be out of sympathy
with the plan for a royal divorce. As for Gardiner, though
he had earlier served as an emissary for Henry at Rome,
he also might show some independence. About his ability
there could be no question; the objection of age could not
be raised in his case; and he had far more experience than
Cranmer. Moreover he had been Bishop of Winchester, one
of the greatest dioceses, for several years. He would have
been the obvious and inevitable choice, except for one fact:

he could not be browbeaten, and he might plead that because of the Pope's order he was unable to act. Therefore the choice fell upon Cranmer.

Almost, but not quite always, Canterbury was given to a man already a bishop. And Cranmer held only the Archdeaconry of Taunton, a sinecure that provided him with an income. As there was no fixed rule about the matter, Cranmer was passed over the heads not only of Gardiner and Tunstall but of all the other English bishops. Henry sent for him for only one reason, as Cranmer well understood.

The appointment was disagreeable to him, not only because of his lack of ambition, but because he knew perfectly well that he would have to do as he was told. Though he now shared Henry's views about the invalidity of his marriage to Katharine of Aragon—as he had shown by offering to debate the matter with anybody—he would have much preferred to act as a free agent, something he saw to be quite impossible. Moreover, there was Margaret at Nuremberg, and it was out of the question for him to start his career as Primate in England if Margaret were allowed to appear. She had to be kept completely out of sight for the present.

King Henry VIII's summons, however, had to be obeyed. But excellent horseman though Cranmer was, quite capable of making the journey to Calais in about half the time he actually took, on one pretext or another he loitered, perhaps all the time hoping that the King's mind would change and that he would decide, after all, to nominate Tunstall or Gardiner or Stokesley of London—and Stokesley was always close at hand—or anybody but himself. The King himself might not trouble his head as to what was said, but Cranmer did not relish the prospect of people commenting all over England that he had been brought home simply and solely to do a certain job. Cranmer was a modest man but he did not relish the prospect of the criticism that would be leveled against him, or the envy he would be sure to arouse.

He took so long a time over his journey, not realizing what new conditions had come into being demanding his presence in London at the earliest possible moment, that Henry VIII sent out other messages to spur him on. As the King knew of his famous horsemanship, it was not safe to invent further pretexts for delay. Besides these messages, though they did not reveal the reason why he should make haste, made him quicken his pace as he drew nearer to Calais. After that, as he was under English eyes, he rode saddle and boots from Dover to London.

Chapter Six

Henry's Breach with Rome

Henry had not set out to effect such a breach; indeed, when the Earl of Wiltshire went abroad (accompanied by Thomas Cranmer) to see what he could effect with the Pope and the Emperor, he had hoped that Charles V could be induced to withdraw his opposition and Clement VII to declare the royal marriage null and void. The ordinary means would have seemed more satisfactory to him than cutting England off from the Roman obedience. But that expedient had already occurred to him as one that in the last resort he should use, and he had cautiously advanced towards it, always hoping that it would not be necessary to take the final step, but preparing for it. Even had Clement VII at the last moment acceded to Henry's demands, it was increasingly clear that the King of England had no intention of going back to the old state of affairs. He would not have had Parliament declare him Head of the Church in England, but he was resolved to diminish Papal authority in the sense that it had been recognized by his predecessors. And since Cranmer's departure Thomas Cromwell had steadily increased his power and influence. Even with Cranmer's nomination as Archbishop of Canterbury Cromwell may have had a great deal to do, for though Anne Boleyn got most of the things she wanted, Henry did not have a very high opinion of her sagacity but had come to rely mainly upon Cromwell for advice.

The acknowledgment by Convocation early in 1531 that Henry VIII was Supreme Head of the Church, qualified by the words "as far as God's Law permits," was ominous, but could be explained away by the clergy as being meaningless, and extended by the King according to his own will. The following year the Pope's Annates had been discontinued by Parliament but the operation of the statute had remained suspended, as perhaps the mere threat would suffice. In late August that same year Archbishop Warham had died and, after some discussion, it had been decided to give his position to Cranmer. In the Spring of 1532 Convocation was forced to make what is called the Submission of the Clergy and Sir Thomas More had been permitted to withdraw to private life, being succeeded by Sir Thomas Audley—a man of a very different stripe—at first not with the title of Chancellor but only that of Keeper of the Seal. Then about January 25, 1533, without obtaining an annulment of his marriage to Katharine from any tribunal the King and Anne Boleyn were secretly married. Cranmer had been called to England to give Henry a divorce.

It must further be remembered that, barely a week after Warham died, Anne, now that she and Henry had the situation well in hand, was given the marquisate of Pembroke and a suitable revenue. Her patent provided that any child of her body—it did not have to be a legitimate child—would inherit from her. It is safe to suppose it was immediately after this that the lady whom many had mistakenly thought was the King's mistress, but who was not, did finally yield

57

to his importunities. While her sister Mary had got nothing, Anne, even if she got nothing else, would be the Marchioness of Pembroke and a richly endowed woman. But now that Warham was dead and Cranmer coming to fill his shoes she counted upon being Queen Anne.

It is hardly remarkable that one who acted as a very highpriced courtesan should demand her fee in advance. What is revealing is that the King who for six or seven years had wished to possess her, now that the possibility had opened at last, should, before he bound himself by a second marriage, want to make sure that Anne could bear a child.* By the time of Cranmer's arrival in England, her pregnancy was beginning to be noticeable. This was why Cranmer was spurred along the road to Calais, why the King had to nominate him Archbishop of Canterbury without delay, and why Cranmer as Archbishop should annul the marriage to Katharine.

The Holy See had not yet delivered any judgment on the validity of Henry's marriage to Katharine. Under the circumstances, the Pope felt obliged to act as though Cranmer's appointment posed no problem. Therefore, though Chapuys sent a warning through the Emperor as to why

* The suggestion that before he married Anne Boleyn Henry made sure that she could bear him a child, is sure to meet with the rejoinder that, though Anne Boleyn was pregnant, nobody knew whether she would bear the *male* child that the King so ardently desired as his heir. It was, as a matter of fact, a female child, the future Queen Elizabeth. But Henry had a conviction (which was of course quite superstitious) that, as all of Katharine's many sons had died at birth, or almost immediately afterward—because of the "childlessness" threatened the incestuous by Leviticus—the new wife would bear him a son. But even if Anne's first child was a girl, he was sure she would soon give him a son to inherit the throne.

Cranmer was being nominated Archbishop, the Pope confirmed the appointment. At Henry's insistence he even was willing to forego the large fees normally paid on such occasions. This of course was not because he had liked Dr. Cranmer when he had met him in Italy; it was a last attempt to placate Henry. Perhaps he hoped that the ordinary diplomatic decencies would be observed and the matter of a divorce in England not rushed through; he did not know of course that Anne was pregnant, and that on her account there was going to be indecent haste.

The Pope sent off the necessary Bulls at once, and they were used in an altogether unique way. A few days before his actual consecration, Cranmer in St. Stephen's Chapel took the obligatory vow of submission to the Pope. Now for the first time in history Cranmer told a select group assembled—and just before taking the vow—that he did not intend to consider himself bound by it. For this perjury we must hold Henry VIII primarily responsible, though of course Cranmer could have refused—probably at the cost of his head. He absolved his conscience with the plea that he had taken legal advice (framed to suit the King), and was assured that this was the right thing to do. Though it is hardly possible to agree with Pollard that the taking of the oath with the announcement that he was going to break it indicates a sensitive rectitude, it may be said that the kind of pressure put on him releases him from some criminality.*

* Strype, in his *Memorials of Thomas Cranmer* (Vol. I, Oxford, 1848), lists those present as Cranmer's witnesses: Watkins, the King's prothonotary, Dr. John Tregonwell, Thomas Bedyll, clerk of the Council, Dr. Richard Gwent, of the archdiocesan court of Canterbury, and John Cocks, the vicar-general. This perjury was brought up against Cranmer at his trial in Oxford in Mary's reign, but was then merely a subsidiary point.

From some, but by no means all. This was on March 26, 1533.

Having been duly consecrated on March 30—at the ceremony he read aloud the oath to the Pope which he had repudiated in advance—on April 11, 1533, Cranmer wrote the King asking permission to do the very thing for which he had specifically been appointed: to try the royal divorce case before his own court. This has sometimes been represented as a piece of the rankest hypocrisy; it was rather a compliance with the forms and as such should be judged.

The letter, which seems groveling to us, was *expected* to be groveling, but cannot be entirely excused on that account, as the request was based on the ground that the widespread discussion of the divorce was bringing disunity to the kingdom. Discussion indeed there was, but the people of England were almost unanimous in siding with Katharine; even the few who did not, detested Anne Boleyn. While it is true that the country would very much have liked a Prince in the line of succession, it was not true at all that there was any likelihood of Mary being opposed as Queen when Henry died. One may pass over Cranmer's pious platitudes as only to be expected, but what does pull one up short with disgust is his promise of impartial justice, for we know the case to have been prejudged in Henry's favor.

For Cranmer to have said that he was writing his letter upon his "bended knees," can be condoned as no more than a form of expression. Even so, what Cranmer wrote was not subservient enough—and it is only fair to remember the subservience of those days—for the letter was sent back to him with revisions in the King's own hand. Now Cranmer changes "bended knees" to "prostrate at the feet of your Majesty" (which to us sounds comical)—of his own accord, so far as we can tell, though of course the terrible Thomas Cromwell may have been at his elbow telling him just what to say. However this may be, Cranmer calls Jesus Christ to witness that his only motive was to try the case truly and impartially.

Dunstable was selected for the hearings for two reasons. One was that Katharine of Aragon was living within easy reach and so would not have a chance to say that she was too far away to present her side of the case; another was that Dunstable, being in the very south of Bedfordshire, could quickly send the King the latest news, for which relays of horses were kept ready. He was nervous, absurdly so, as he was now sure of getting his divorce; the most that Katharine could do was to delay the judgment a short while by answering the court summons that was sent her. On the advice of Chapuys she ignored it completely as her cause was still pending before the Holy See, and she might have weakened the force of her appeal had she presented herself at Dunstable. Since she did not go, the matter was rushed through with the utmost speed—even though the forms of canon law were punctiliously observed—so that on May 17 Cranmer was able to pronounce the marriage of Henry and Katharine null and void on the ground of its being incestuous.

All this time Cranmer was aware that Henry and Anne had been married on or about January 25. That she was well advanced in pregnancy he and everybody else could see from her figure. Nevertheless, as soon as he got back to London he issued another statement: that the marriage of the King and Anne Boleyn was "good"—that is, valid, as of course it was if the earlier marriage had been really incestuous. But no precise statement was ever issued as to the date of the second marriage, and to this day we do not know positively who celebrated it, though several likely guesses have been made.

Still another detail had to be attended to: Anne's coronation. This was something which, strictly speaking, was not necessary, as Henry VIII was the reigning sovereign. But since, in his youthful uxoriousness, he had had Katharine crowned with himself, Anne demanded a coronation, too. In this she showed her lack of judgment, for the crowds in the London streets that day showed by their sullenness that she was unpopular, though usually they made any kind of spectacle the opportunity for a frolic. About all she got out of it was that, according to tradition, she spent the night before the ceremony in the Tower in the royal apartments —the very same apartments she occupied when, in 1536, she was sent to the Tower to be beheaded—and that the King provided gaily decorated barges and floats and trumpeters to take her part of the way to Westminster Abbey.

There were many gorgeously clad nobles in the coronation procession, and Cranmer made a grand figure on the horse he rode to the Abbey, for he was to crown her. As she could hardly wear the white silk of a virgin, she was clad in vivid scarlet, and she wore her hair (of which she was proud) unbound, so that it fell down her long neck to her shoulders and even to her waist. But not even she or her father or brother divined that tragedy was not very far away; least of all did Cranmer, who had come into his eminence solely because of her.

What of course followed, as soon as the news reached Rome that Cranmer had given a decree of nullity, was an instant breach with the Papacy. However, it would have been possible to patch this up and on several occasions it seemed to be close to the point of happening. Interdicts and excommunications were not new things, so when excommunications were issued in this case, their application was put in abeyance. Clement VII was not a strong Pope and he did not realize that the day had already passed when Papal thunderbolts were going to be of much effect. Yet he brandished them with one hand, meanwhile holding out the other in friendship; there could hardly have been a worse way for a Pope to comport himself with a man like Henry VIII.

In March, 1534, Parliament passed the first Act of Supremacy, obligating everybody to whom it applied to take an oath recognizing the King as Head of the Church. Further "teeth" were put into the statute at the end of the year. But with such matters, since they were of a political nature, Cranmer had relatively little to do, except that as a bishop he voted as required in the House of Lords. However, though some members of Parliament voted as they did solely or mainly because of the pressure the King brought to bear, one must say of Cranmer that the abrogation of the Roman obedience completely coincided with his own beliefs as to what should be done. For that matter England was still Catholic, except for eccentric heretics here and there, all of whom took good care to conceal opinions that were out of the ordinary. But England was not, generally speaking, enthusiastic about Papal authority, even though a good many believed (without openly saying so) that the King had no right to appropriate this authority for himself.

For some time Thomas Cromwell had been exercising many of the powers possessed by Cardinal Wolsey, though he was only a layman. The King, except perhaps in his early years, was a good deal more than the playboy he seemed to be, though even now in his maturity those in charge of the administration were well advised to see that Henry had plenty of free time for his various amusements. Of these administrators by far the most important was Cromwell, who in 1535 was appointed the King's Vicar-general, all the bishops being promptly informed that since the King, who was now in charge of the Church, did not have time to give his attention to every detail, they should report everything to the man acting on his behalf. Cromwell even sharply reproved Cranmer when he ventured to use his title of Primate. If Henry was now Pope in England, Cromwell was the vice-Pope.

A new era had in fact arrived, a revolution had been effected. And though the Henrician system has received various modifications, it is still with us. Henry had rebelled against the Pope, and Cromwell devised various drastic means for the extirpation of the Papal Supremacy; yet it was Thomas Cranmer, the patient and affable and unobtrusive, who was really the builder of England's new religion—though mainly after Henry himself had passed from the scene. It is to Cranmer that Anglicanism in the various forms in which we know it, owes its greatest debt.

Chapter Seven

The Oath of Supremacy

The royal supremacy over the Church had been admitted, after a fashion, by Convocation—first the Convocation of Canterbury and then that of York—but with a qualification which could be considered as rendering it innocuous. Though Parliament took stronger action against the Pope later, it did not give statutory force to Henry's claim to be Supreme Head of the Church in England until the Spring of 1534. Then, of course, what Convocation had done earlier was used as justification, but more was read into it than was ever meant. Had the assembly of the clergy stood firm in 1531, the King would have been nonplused; he could not have put the entire priesthood of England into jail. But they were as a class placable and even timid men, and to their eventual, complete subjugation to the Crown they put up no resistance. Thomas Cranmer had nothing to do with all this, for he was not even a member of Convocation, and at that time he was abroad. The main thing that he did was the act for which he had been made Archbishop of Canterbury: to pronounce the decree of nullity of the King's first marriage.

The Dunstable divorce had been the decisive fact; the coronation that followed, which should have been for Anne an occasion of radiant joy, was rather a day of humiliation, except that, after all, the crown had been placed on her head and the courtiers by whom she was surrounded gave her almost enough flattery to make her forget the morose attitude of the London populace that had watched her procession going to the Abbey. There the monks were in attendance, as were the bishops and the nobles. All people of prominence quite understood that now they had better ingratiate themselves with the new Queen.

There were however a few people who were not willing to pretend to be complaisant. Thus Sir Thomas More, until recently the Lord Chancellor and well aware of what was expected of him, knowing that his absence would be remarked and bring about Queen Anne's enmity, refused to be present. Several of his friends among the bishops—among them Tunstall of Durham and Veysey of Exeter—virtually tried to drag him to the Abbey for the coronation by sending him £20 for a robe suitable for such an occasion. It was useless; More stayed away, and when he met the bishops afterwards merely jested on the subject. He knew that they shared his views; as events were soon to prove, they did not share his courage.

Little time was lost—even before the passing of the Act of Succession—to prepare a weapon against all who were considered likely to refuse the oath it exacted. It so happened that for some years past in a convent in Canterbury there had lived a young nun whom many people believed (and the nun for a while believed it herself) to have visions and auditions and a gift of prophecy. She had had an interview with the King himself; she had also met Bishop Fisher of Rochester and Sir Thomas More. But where More showed that he had no faith in her claims, Bishop Fisher unfortunately gave her some countenance, for which he paid dearly, only escaping with his life when an act of attainder was

66

passed against him. He was, however, given a fine equal to a year's revenue of his diocese.

But first of course the young nun—Elizabeth Barton, sometimes called the Maid of Kent—had to be convicted of treason. (The treason in her case consisted in saying that the King would die within seven months if he married Anne Boleyn. To speak of the King's death at all could be regarded as treasonable; in this instance the rather unbalanced young woman also showed that she did not have the gift of prophecy.) Under instructions from Cromwell, Cranmer sent for her—as he was her Ordinary—and asked her a number of routine questions. His manner was disarming, but it seems hardly fair to accuse him of being a crafty police agent of the Nazi or Soviet type, for he was entitled to be informed as to her doings, and a woman as foolish as this would probably have given the same answers to anybody. She said more than enough to get sent to the Tower, where, however, she was not tortured to extract damaging answers (there was no need for that) but instead treated almost as though she were a great lady. What was demanded of her was that she make a public confession at Paul's Cross that she was an impostor. This was probably more than she need have said; it would be much nearer the truth to say that she had first deluded herself and was persuaded to make her claims by a group of priests who had taken her up as a protegée. Sir Thomas More was among the crowd which heard her make her confession, and wrote to Cromwell congratulating him for exposing a fraud. Elizabeth Barton had done no great harm to anybody, but Cromwell continued to detain her in the Tower, for he perceived that he might use her to incriminate others, including Katharine of Aragon, just as he used her to incriminate Fisher. Besides, he thought that she and her "accomplices" (for so they were termed) could be dealt with in such a way as to terrify those who refused to take the Oath of Submission into abandoning their obstinacy. If Fisher and More, the men chiefly aimed at, still refused the oath, the Nun of Kent and her accomplices would be sent to Tyburn. On the other hand, had Fisher and More done what was required of them, Elizabeth Barton and her friends would almost certainly have been released, as they were now discredited.

Sir Thomas More was told that he had to appear at Lambeth Palace on April 12, 1534, along with Fisher and some of the more prominent of the London clergy, to take the Oath of Submission. Most of them did so without any qualms —indeed, in a festive spirit, freely partaking of the drink provided for them. More noted that Hugh Latimer, soon to be a bishop and twenty years later one of the Marian martyrs, took several of the men with whom he was around the neck "so handsomely that, had they been women I would have weened that he was wanton." There too was the Vicar of Croydon, ready enough to take the oath, the same man who, upon the publication of More's famous book in 1516, took it in a sense that was never intended and amused people by asking that he be sent to Utopia to convert its admirable inhabitants.

Sir Thomas More was vastly entertained by what he saw that day and wrote a vivid account of it, but regarding himself and the demanded oath he was quietly firm. He told the Commissioners before whom he appeared that, while he was willing enough to swear to the Act of Succession— which made the children of Anne the King's heirs, instead of the Princess Mary, who was naturally bastardized when

her parents' marriage was pronounced incestuous by Cranmer
—he could not in conscience swear to the Preamble, since
that definitely rejected the Pope's authority. He was treated
very courteously by the Commissioners—who included
Audley, the man who had stepped into More's shoes, Cromwell, Benson, the Abbot of Westminster and Cranmer himself—but as he refused to do what they wanted, they suggested that he take a walk in the palace grounds and give
the matter further thought. He returned only to say that
he remained of the same opinion, whereupon he was sent
to the Tower.

Cranmer, who respected More's scholarship and his high
character, came forward with a suggestion which has sometimes been thought merely crafty but which probably was
a kindly effort to provide More with a means of escape. At
least one must grant that Cranmer's proposed formula was
ingenious: it was that More and Fisher swear only to the
Act itself; then people could be counted upon to take it
for granted that the stricter oath had been taken. Just to
give out, "Oh, yes; they have taken the oath" could suffice.
But though More was perfectly willing to accept this solution, Henry (or Cromwell) considered it inadvisable, for
if the complete truth later emerged, it might be damaging
to the King. One cannot blame Henry VIII for insisting
upon a completely unqualified adhesion, but neither should
we seek to make Cranmer shifty for trying to find a way
out of the difficulty. He was a good-natured man, and though
he may never have met Sir Thomas More before this occasion, he had read his books with admiration. Fisher he
must have known in the days when he himself was a Fellow of Jesus College and Bishop Fisher the Chancellor of
Cambridge University. The Archbishop wished no harm to

either, though no doubt he thought they were being over-scrupulous.

The charming and gay-hearted Sir Thomas was a favorite with everybody, as he had been in better days even with Henry VIII. But Fisher—gentle, saintly, learned, revered but with a belligerent core—was pursued with rancor, and several dark suspicions have been directed at the Boleyn family, though this is not to say that they have been proved. What is, however, a fact is this: in 1531 an act of Parliament was passed which directed that poisoners (or those who attempted poison) should be put to death by being boiled in oil, and this statute specifically named a certain Richard Rouse, who had been a cook employed by Fisher, as one who was to suffer in this way. Rouse admitted (whether under torture or not we do not know) that somebody had given him a powder to put in the soup that was to be served in Fisher's house at dinner. Several of the guests were made ill in consequence but nobody actually died. The name of the man who gave Rouse the powder was hushed up, but Rouse himself died in boiling oil. The King was worked up because if a bishop could be poisoned so could a king. But it was suspected that the Boleyn family were implicated and were being protected.

Nothing is definitely known, but all the circumstances of Rouse's case suggest that behind him were powerfully placed people whose misdeeds were being covered up. It also remains a mystery where the ball came from that was shot across the river at the Bishop's house. All one can say is that the trajectory showed it came from the general direction of the Boleyn's house. Finally, there is the fact that Chapuys believed that Katharine of Aragon died from the effects of slow poison (which was certainly not the case) and that after Anne Boleyn's fall Henry himself openly said that she had removed his bastard son by poison, and that she was trying to poison his daughter Mary as well. No charge was ever preferred about poison, and one can only say that it was common in that age to attribute the death of almost every important personage to this cause (nearly always without the slightest proof), so that we cannot treat such things seriously. They are mentioned only to indicate the kind of reputation the Boleyns had, not to say that they deserved it.

There were, however, a number of judicial murders. Thus when three Carthusian Priors went to Cromwell to ask him, rather naïvely, what course of action they should follow with regard to the Act of Supremacy (by this time further teeth had been put in it which made it treason maliciously to deny the King any of his titles), he instantly had them arrested and brought to speedy trial. The three Priors—and with them a Brigittine monk of Syon and a secular priest— were found guilty, but only after Cromwell had sent the jury a message as to what verdict they should bring in. When they still hesitated to convict, because of the word "maliciously" that Parliament had deliberately inserted into the statute to protect such men as these, he went into the jury-room himself to threaten the jurors with the direst penalties.

No doubt the Carthusians would have been executed in any event. But it was also hoped that their execution would terrify More and Fisher into taking the oath. This was the technique followed the previous year, when on April 21, 1534, Elizabeth Barton and her "accomplices" were sent to Tyburn, which was obviously done in the expectation that, after that, the two illustrious recalcitrants would yield. Cromwell probably hoped that by sending to the gallows a batch of obscure people who meant nothing to him he could save the lives of two men of the loftiest reputation. For Cromwell, ruthless though he was, was kind enough when he could afford to be so. No doubt this is a rather strange way of showing kindness, but he had no animus against Fisher and his feelings were friendly towards More.

The two men were kept in the Tower a long time—about fifteen months—and, except towards the end, were well treated and were permitted to have special food sent in, to read and write as much as they liked, and to take exercise in the Tower gardens. But each man continued to stand upon the same technicality: that they could not be touched so long as they maintained a strict silence about their opinions. As there was always the possibility of a resort to torture, More took the precaution of sending out messages to friends that, if they ever heard that his mind had changed, they were to understand that this was only because he had been put upon the rack. Fortunately that was a point at which Cromwell drew the line in their case.

The means employed were of a different kind. Several times commissions visited them, to see what might be accomplished by persuasion, or, if persuasion failed, to catch some unguarded expression which might suffice for bringing them to trial. Cromwell usually headed these commissions, and Cranmer was several times drawn upon, because his courteous and affable manners might be very serviceable. Cranmer—indeed, all the visitors—always wished the prisoners well, and did their best to induce them to be reasonable. Fisher was non-committal but grave; More, on the other hand, was equally noncommittal but was full of stories and jests. With neither man was any headway made.

The Carthusian Priors had, after all, implied by asking Cromwell's advice that they had no intention of submission, and Cromwell contrived to read malice into this. But it was hard to see how men could be accused of malice who said nothing at all. Neither prisoner had much faith that this would be of permanent help, but so long as it could be used, they used it for all it was worth.

At last Cromwell fell back upon barefaced lying (and one hopes it was not with the knowledge and consent of Henry) when he sent the Solicitor-general and future Chancellor, Sir Richard Rich to Fisher, to tell him that More had taken the oath, and to More to tell him that Fisher had done the same thing. Each man evaded the trap by simple fidelity to principle: whatever anybody else may have done, it made no difference to the question at issue.

But the base resources of the administration were still not exhausted. John Fisher was informed that Henry, as King, sought his candid opinion on the case, in his capacity as bishop, and he could give this without fear, as immunity was guaranteed. Thus appealed to, Fisher felt that it was his duty to speak—and at once the trap was sprung. On June 17, 1535, Fisher was tried in Westminster Hall and five days later was executed. The new Pope, in an attempt to appease Henry, had shortly before this announced that the Bishop of Rochester was to be created Cardinal. The action only further infuriated the King against a man who had been a friend of his grandmother. Had Fisher not been so old and ill, he would have been dragged on a hurdle to Tyburn to be hanged, drawn and quartered, with all the rest of the ghastly embellishments of that mode of execution. But as it was thought that he might die on the hurdle if this was attempted, he was given the more merciful death

73

of decapitation on Tower Hill. The execution of the Carthusian Priors was, however, carried out at Tyburn with all the usual barbarities on the nineteenth of the same month, and they were executed in their religious habits, to give further emphasis to the royal wrath. More knew by now that his own time had come.

The King and his advisers were convinced they could no longer delay in breaking the back of resistance, not being too scrupulous as to what methods they used; everybody should know who was now master in England. In its way —or from the royal point of view—the policy was sound. It was common knowledge that many who had taken the oath were at heart pro-Papal still; therefore intimidation had to be used. When the Brigittine monk who was tried with the Carthusian Priors was asked who were the people who thought as he did, he gave the answer, "All good men," but when pressed further kept silence lest he incriminate others. Similarly Sir Thomas More, writing his *Dialogue of Comfort* in the Tower, very broadly hinted at much the same thing but would name nobody. It was not for him to be the government's gratuitous informer.

Despite his incarceration, More contrived to be well posted about a good many things. Thus, early in 1535, when he was still allowed to walk in the Tower gardens with his favorite daughter, Margaret Roper, whose husband was his first biographer, Sir Thomas asked how the Queen was and received the answer, "In faith, father, never better." To this came the sad rejoinder, "Never better, Meg! Alas, Meg, alas! It pitieth me to remember into what misery, poor soul, she shall shortly come." In this More spoke not as a prophet but out of his knowledge of men, and of King

74

Henry in particular. Apparently some rumors had reached him that the King was tired of Anne already.

The means used to find evidence against More were different from those used in Fisher's case, but were no less disgraceful. Sir Richard Rich came to his cell, accompanied by two men named Palmer and Southwell, who were to truss up the books of which More was now to be deprived. In the course of talk Rich put some hypothetical questions to which More made noncommittal answers. Yet on the day of the trial in Westminster Hall soon afterwards Rich gave a completely different version of what was said, appearing as a witness though he was the prosecutor—a gross impropriety—and called upon Palmer and Southwell for corroboration. Neither man dared contradict Rich, yet each was too ashamed to say that Rich's testimony was right; so they squirmed out of their difficulty by muttering that they had paid little attention to what was said, as at the time they were busy making bundles of the books. This also means that, even on the supposition that Rich had reported the conversation accurately, the evidence was insufficient, for the law required that in treason cases two witnesses were necessary.

Upon this the prisoner at the bar roundly accused the prosecutor of being a downright liar, and one, moreover, whose character was well known to all the members of the court. Despite this of course More was conducted out of Westminster Hall with the ax-heads turned outward. But after sentence had been pronounced Thomas More spoke out in plain terms and with an eloquence which still rings. As for Rich, he became Chancellor under Edward VI, turning his coat when Queen Mary came to the throne and turning it again under Queen Elizabeth.

75

One would like to give more time to what is the classic case of Tudor criminology; but the life of More is not being written, so it need only be said that Sir Thomas More died on July 6th with characteristic bonhomie, jesting even on the scaffold, before making his famous brief speech—"The King's good servant, but God's first." What it shows is that Henry VIII was all the more incensed by the fact that More had been his friend—perhaps the only friend the King ever had, as contrasted with boon-companions—and was determined to break down all opposition. But a thrill of horror ran throughout Europe, and was no doubt felt by Dr. Cranmer, though he was careful not to say anything, any more than he did when his patroness, Anne Boleyn, was beheaded on Tower Hill less than a year later.

Thomas Cranmer, except for deplorable behavior at the time of Anne Boleyn's fall, took no part in these bloody proceedings, except that he several times went with the commissioners who tried to persuade this prisoner or that to change his mind. He was a kindly man but not a very effectual one; yet one must say that though his mild attempts to obtain mercy for those marked down as victims received scant attention from Cromwell and the King, it surely is better to seem bumbling, or even absurd, than to be callous and correct and efficiently cruel. Cranmer was well aware that there was nothing much that he could do to prevent the exaction of what was called justice, but that he tried to do anything at all is to his credit.

Cranmer, in short, was rapidly discovering what his position really was—Archbishop of Canterbury, but also the lackey of the overpowering men above him. Even so, he probably was not brought to a full comprehension of this until the fall of Anne Boleyn in the late Spring of 1536.

During Edward's reign he regained some part of the power that he had supposed was attached to his office, though even then he could act only with the consent of those in control of the country. It was not until Mary's reign that he at last emerged—though still subject to sudden tremors of alarm—with some dignity and manliness. One is inclined to ascribe the truculence he displayed then, at an injudicious moment, to the fact that he had often been ruthlessly trampled upon by the vigorous and vengeful. Though he had never sought the position into which he was shoved, somewhat to his dismay, he was hurt and surprised to discover that he was mainly for ceremonial use. Therefore when his last chance came he was firm though frightened, not prepared to confess his total inadequacy. Therefore, too, the heroic end that was so astonishing.

Chapter Eight

The Plundering of
the Monks

Cromwell, it will be remembered, had received a training in the suppression of religious houses when he was in the service of Cardinal Wolsey. But the suppression which he started to make, as the Vicar-general of Henry VIII, the latter as Head of the Church in England, ended in the total extirpation of monasticism in England, whereas what Wolsey had done affected no more than about thirty institutions and was by permission of the Pope. Even Cromwell at first operated under restrictions imposed by the act of Parliament of 1536, and Parliament had no intention of wholesale destruction but rather of only mending some manifest defects. If it did not stay at that point very long, this was because greed, once aroused, could not be restrained.

Cranmer was willing enough for these matters to be handled by Cromwell, especially because from the start it was clear that the methods employed were of a rough and ready, not to say an unsavory sort, ruthless, rapacious and venal. While on a few occasions Cranmer did try to protect a religious community—the cathedral priory of Canterbury being an instance—he was made to understand that a more general interference would not be brooked. If he or members of his family were given one or two small pieces of the loot, this was because it was thought advisable to placate (and implicate) the Archbishop. But broadly speaking, Cranmer's part in the first phase of the Reformation in England was that of a spectator who did not approve of everything that was done.

Cromwell very shrewdly judged that permanence could be assured the expropriations by implicating many people in what was done. He had assured Henry VIII at first that he would make him the richest king in Christendom, and the King at first imagined this meant he could add the whole of the loot to the royal endowments. But Cromwell managed to convince him that the loot should be shared; otherwise he was not likely to get permission (if it can be called that) of Parliament to do the looting, and would afterwards hold his Supremacy insecurely. Henry may have been a bit rueful about this, but he was brought to admit the soundness of Cromwell's wisdom. In any event the monastic plunder would have been squandered, just as the King had squandered the immense fortune left him by his parsimonious father.

The argument was advanced that the revenues of the monasteries, which were pictured as much greater than they really were, because of a multitude of various drains made upon the monks, would be put to much better use by the Crown. Never again would there be any need of war subsidies; and roads, schools, hospitals, bridges, dikes against the sea could all be provided for, still leaving the King with a large surplus for emergencies. Theoretically this may have been so, if the King could have appropriated the whole of the monastic wealth, though a spendthrift like Henry VIII was the last person in the world to be trusted with such wealth. The very fact that he had run through the fortune left him by his father, was the best of reasons for not giving him another fortune to waste. From his point of view, however, the very fact that his coffers were rapidly being emptied was a reason he should find means of filling them again.

The idea of suppressing the monasteries was by no means new. During the reign of Henry IV proposals along somewhat similar lines had been presented to Parliament by Lord Cobham (otherwise known as Sir John Oldcastle) but were soon shown to be ludicrous. He was not merely regarded as an eccentric but was execrated, and his odium lasted so long that Shakespeare first introduced Falstaff under the name of Cobham. His scheme called for creating and endowing a large number of peers and knights, with the idea that these would be of military value to the King; Cromwell's scheme was that a variety of secular works, excellent in themselves, be supported, though this shows the low value Cromwell placed on religion. Nevertheless, had the hospitals, schools and the rest appeared, many would have said that he was a far-sighted statesman. As it is, everybody must agree that even the opportunity for secular benefits was thrown away, and that the main result was the aggrandizement of those already rich, the creation of more rich men, and (as against this) the weakening of the Crown.

Before the troubles of Henry's reign took their really serious turn two books appeared which bore upon much the same theme, and both of which were trenchantly answered by Sir Thomas More. One, written by a lawyer under the pseudonym of Christopher St. German, was rather an attack upon the clergy and professed to have as author a man perfectly orthodox, as possibly he was. It was not primarily an attack on monasticism, so perhaps it would be as well to restrict our attention to the other book, Simon Fish's *Supplication of Beggars*. Even that was rather a complaint that vast sums of money were wasted upon Masses for the dead, and so brought in all the clergy, though no doubt monks and friars received the greater part of these Mass stipends. The title of More's rejoinder, *The Supplication of Souls,* indicates the line he took: that the souls in Purgatory, the "poor souls," are in dire need of the prayers of those still on earth. Of course he had no difficulty in pulling to shreds Fish's fantastic estimate that the monasteries possessed half the wealth of the country. It was probably closer to a quarter, though of course even that was a great deal.

It is worth noting that these books did not accuse the religious of immorality so much as of covetousness and sloth. As for that, Dean Colet, who until his death in 1519 was Sir Thomas More's confessor, in a sermon preached before the Convocation of Canterbury, gave the clergy of his day a grand wigging, without mincing any words. He does not mention immoral conduct as among their faults, which indicates that it must have been so rare it was not worth including in his diatribe: his reproof is all directed against such matters as that many of the clergy—and few of these could have been monks—wasted their time in alehouses, or dicing, and similar amusements. This might not have been very reprehensible in other men but was certainly not fitting to parish priests.

That the suppression of the monasteries was in the air we know from some hints dropped in letters by Chapuys, the Imperial Ambassador. Fish's book, advocating suppression—there is some reason to believe it was circulated with Henry VIII's connivance—appeared in 1529. And though

81

More said he did not know of anybody favorable to it, it may have been because he chose his friends carefully, or because men who secretly did hanker to obtain some of the monastic lands would hardly have announced this to More, or because, in the year that Fish wrote, they would probably have been careful to keep such opinions to themselves. If there was anything amiss with the English monasteries, they were given ample time to reform themselves before the storm came.

It was, however, insinuated then, and at the time of the suppression openly used as an argument, that the Crown would become at a stroke so rich that no taxes would ever have to be asked for again. The prospect of great public works was also dangled as a bait. Finally there was the odium that had become attached to the clerical body. The exactions that were so greatly resented were made by ecclesiastical courts of which monks were very seldom members, but the resentment was made to apply to monasticism. Only now and then did people stop to think that, as landlords, monks were, generally speaking, easy-going, and to consider the many benefits they conferred upon the poor. Or perhaps these benefits seemed less than what the country would gain if the monks went. Yet upon the whole the monasteries were popular with ordinary people; it was those who counted upon getting some share of the plunder—the nobles and officials—who were bent upon the destruction.

There was no necessary connection between Henry VIII's breach with the Papacy and what was done to the monasteries, and when that breach occurred probably most Englishmen supposed that, though it was a quarrel of exceptional violence, it would be only temporary. Anne lasted an even shorter time than was expected, and as Katharine of Aragon died almost simultaneously, there was nothing whatever to prevent Henry from taking a third wife (which in fact he did within a couple of weeks), and from doing so as a Catholic in good standing. Though by that time the plundering of the monasteries had already begun, the process could have been checked and a concordat worked out with the Holy See.

That some religious houses were not well administered was notorious. Others had declined greatly in numbers. In others again the discipline had grown rather lax. Henry— who had a wonderful faculty for deceiving himself—said he intended to suppress only those houses which had ceased to be useful; their inmates could be transferred to better run institutions, thus strengthening rather than weakening monasticism. His intentions were professedly noble; he was going to reform. And a reform must be said to have been desirable, providing it was genuine.

Perhaps at the outset the motives were for the most part sincere, except that Cromwell almost certainly intended to get rid of religious houses as part of the clear and definite policy he had set before himself. But had he ventured to unveil all that was in his mind, he would not have found the statutory support he needed. The act of 1536 therefore explicitly said that in the larger religious houses God was well served, that they had an adequate number of monks or nuns for the choral chanting of the Divine Office, and that their spiritual state was excellent. All that was proposed was to transfer members of failing religious houses to these larger houses (with the endowment needed for their maintenance), whereupon the Crown would take possession of monastic manors now no longer needed. To this proposition most of the larger abbeys agreed readily enough,

thinking the adjustment would work for their own benefit and for the benefit of monasticism in general.

There were, however, some things in the Act that makes
one wonder how much sincerity there was in the Parliamentary mind. It was not at all unreasonable that a minimum
of twelve religious should be declared as indispensable for
the rendering of the choral Office in solemnity. But that
the standard for measuring the good discipline of the mon-
astery or convent should be its possessing £200 a year in
revenue—that is, in such rents as it received, and the amount
should be multiplied by at least 25 to give a modern ap-
proximation—surely must have been thought arbitrary and
absurd by most members of Parliament. If disorders occurred in any of these houses—and human nature being
what it is, there must have been disorders now and then—
we can be sure it was those houses with most money to
squander on pleasant vices which were likely to be least
edifying. This is, of course, not to suggest that the larger
houses, just because they had ample endowments, contained
no members who were slothful, arrogant or given up to the
kinds of things with which monks have so often been charged.
But it is sheer nonsense to say that good religious discipline
inevitably follows wealth. It is even more nonsensical to
say that because a religious house is not well off financially,
it is bound to be corrupt. We may be quite sure that many
a small community, despite monetary difficulties, carried out
its religious duties in most exemplary fashion. Only when it
had got into such a pass that discipline broke down was
there any real justification for suppression.

There is no need to pretend that all monasteries and convents, whether rich or poor, with many members or few,
were as edifying as they should have been. To say this would

be to fall into the absurdity of ignoring that, taking men and women as a whole, among a certain number we must expect irregularity of one sort and another, even including downright immorality now and then. But it is anomalous to run across serious misconduct of any kind among people who must have started out with the intention of dedicating their lives to God, though some of them will lose their first fervor and lapse into what is not consonant with their original ideals. I submit that what is being said here is only plain common sense, and allows both for good intentions and for human frailty. In any event, to use the income that the community happens to possess as a yardstick is so ridiculous that it need only be mentioned for the average person to admit the point without further argument.

We know that Cromwell and his agents brandished over these smaller religious houses the threat of suppression as a means of extracting bribes. Of those that could be suppressed only about half were actually suppressed during this first stage of the process; the rest were allowed to continue (they imagined the continuation would be permanent) if they paid well enough to satisfy the King's Vicar-general and the kind of men he employed as his agents. Cromwell had done the same thing when he was employed by Cardinal Wolsey; now under Henry VIII he had vastly augmented powers, and these were used to the full. We know this from documentary evidence—though there is no space to produce it here; for we find that Drs. Leigh and Layton, the chief of his agents, were frequently writing to Cromwell complaining against one another, and that Cromwell was frequently placated by presents, which might be money, a bowl of gold, or a fine horse. If the religious houses were, in fact, corrupt, they were corrupted in a new kind of way, that of being obliged to satisfy venality.

Nor was this all: sometimes young men would be sent to a convent (ostensibly as agents to improve them) where they made improper advances to the younger nuns or asked questions that were shockingly indecent. Nor was there much use in the Sisters complaining to Cromwell; then the agents found it the easiest thing in the world to deny the stories, or else to answer that the complaints showed what dirty minds these nuns had. More often, some querulous monk or nun was found who, disgruntled with his or her Superior, said something that could be twisted into what was never intended at all. Furthermore, some who could be induced to bring specific charges were rewarded with small pensions, while the rest were turned out into the world with hardly more than the clothes on their backs. Too often this was the reward given to the religious who met all the tricks with a disdainful silence. It is really remarkable that those who, according to the standards invented by the agents, were one way or another not all that they should have been, had their corruption paid for with a pension, while those who would say nothing were pitilessly turned adrift. It is not being suggested that this state of affairs was general, or that there was a clear code of rules by which the religious were everywhere judged—for caprice as well as hard cash entered into the matter—but it did count a great deal when a monk or nun was found who was willing to be "co-operative."

After the so-called rising of 1537 known as the Pilgrimage of Grace—really only a protest on the part of the people of Lincolnshire and the North, and with it the religious had next to nothing to do—Cromwell abandoned all pretense of keeping within the limits of the Act of 1536. After that he charged that the larger monasteries, those which had been singled out for praise by the Parliamentary statute, were also sinks of iniquity. Against them he also threatened to proceed, on the grounds that (as he alleged) they had given some supplies to the Pilgrims, which probably did happen in some cases, and which might make them traitors to the King. These larger monasteries had all been wiped out by the time of Cromwell's own fall in 1540.

In some instances, however, if there was a ready compliance with the royal will, and a "voluntary surrender" was made, benefices were often conferred—in a few instances even bishoprics on the Abbots—whereas other Abbots, like those of Glastonbury, Reading and Colchester, were hanged at the abbey gate. The monks of such communities as had done what was demanded of them, were, when possible, made into Prebendaries of a cathedral; and some Abbots, for whom no fitting benefices were immediately available, were given very comfortable houses and adequate incomes. The fact was ignored that no abbey was the personal possession of the Abbot but was equally the property of all the monks; if an Abbot signed prudently on the dotted line, Cromwell treated the abbey as actually belonging to the Abbot, this being the most expeditious way of dealing with the case. But all the monks of a wealthy religious house were looked after when they were accommodating, and as the poor fellows had to live in some way or other, the great majority fell into line, receiving a benefice if one was available, but in the majority of instances no more than a small pension that would barely support them.

The loot of course was enormous, though not nearly as large as had been expected, only about £320,000 a year (the reader must again be reminded to multiply that figure by at least 25 to arrive at some concept of its modern value). A large part of this had to be given outright, or in exchange for some secular holding of comparatively little value; and a process was begun which by no means ended with Henry VIII but perhaps showed its most sordid features under the greedy politicians who governed England during the time when his young son Edward VI sat on the throne and did as he was told. Henry was a pious man, and though he never got around to founding many new bishoprics and endowing them out of what had been filched from the monks, he did found two or three, only to have them suppressed by those in command in Edward's time (men who also greatly pared down the diocesan holdings—they sometimes placed a bishop upon a relatively small salary and pocketed the rest of the endowments themselves).

The Act of 1536 was passed largely upon the evidence which is supposed to have been presented to Parliament in a "Black Book." One can only say that such a book simply does not exist and could only have been a summary of the *comperta* issued by Cromwell's agents. In any event the reports sent in by the agents have been subject to close examination and have often been shown to be quite unreliable. The agents are known to have been men of a low character—as was Cromwell himself—and though their reports to their employer need not be dismissed as a mere pack of lies, they did all too frequently contain lies, or what the agents were told out of terror or the hope of a reward. In short the agents almost invariably said what they knew they were expected to say; if they did not obtain what they were looking for, they had a number of means of extorting it. While we need not question that they did sometimes find things that were amiss in the religious houses, there can

88

be no doubt that the creatures sent out exaggerated grossly for no other purpose than to vilify the monks and nuns (unless a fat bribe was forthcoming). Hardly anything they reported is to be accepted, unless it receives corroboration from other sources.

Thomas Cranmer may be said to have played an important role, despite his intentions, in the suppression of the monasteries in England. His appointment as Archbishop of Canterbury made the breach with Rome inevitable, and was, indeed, Henry VIII's indication that he had decided upon that breach. Even so, the breach in itself did not mean the extirpation of the monasteries, for these, in fact, were left unmolested for a couple of years and were not all expropriated until seven years later. Even though no doubt some sort of adjustment was fairly certain to have occurred, adjustment need not have involved destruction. It was even possible that within the Henrician system monasticism might have been permitted to continue indefinitely. It was Thomas Cromwell, the man who managed matters during those years, who persuaded the King that the royal Supremacy was not safe so long as the religious Orders were left alone. What weighed most with the King and the majority of the nobles surrounding him was the monastic wealth which would be appropriated by the Crown—first, part of it, and then, as greed grew by what it fed upon, the whole of that wealth.

Cranmer, while no doubt he approved in a general way of monastic reorganization—and perhaps even of total expropriation—cannot be blamed for the policy adopted, and the methods by which this was effected must have shocked him. Upon the whole, he should be regarded as a spectator of what was done, sometimes approving but sometimes apprehensive, if not disgusted, by this or that feature of the process. But it was a matter not left in his hands, though as a member of the Council he cannot be absolved from all responsibility or some share of the guilt attaching to what was done. But if it comes to that, some of the Abbots who were members of the House of Lords, like many Bishops of the conservative sort, made and could make, no very effective protest, even had they wished to. All were now directly subject to the King, even in ecclesiastical matters; and as Cromwell was the King's Vicar-general they had to obey Cromwell. Even in Convocation, Thomas Cromwell or his representative presided, for, as the historian Bishop Stubbs was later to put it, Henry, "with regard to the Church of England [wished to be] the pope, the whole pope, and something more than the pope." He and Cromwell must be considered the villains of the piece.

A final fact must be mentioned that may serve partially to exculpate Thomas Cranmer: even bishops of Catholic leanings—men like Gardiner of Winchester, and Tunstall and Bonner—were careful not to appear as opponents of the piogram decided upon. For this there seemed a good reason, though one must say that it showed little heroism. They looked for the quarrel between the King of England and the Pope to blow itself out in a few years. Then they wished to be on hand to lead a restoration. But it must be candidly said that such men, even when they hoped that England would return to the Roman obedience, had little hope that the old state of things would return just as it had been before. Some modifications had to be expected. As for monasticism, while such men might have hoped for an atmosphere in which a few of the old abbeys would be allowed to come back, and with them perhaps a few new monasteries, the former system had passed beyond recovery. In any case it was only incidental to Catholicism.

Chapter Nine

Cranmer and Anne Boleyn

It was the notice of the King that Thomas Cranmer apparently attracted first. But before Henry advanced him at all it may be supposed that he had first consulted Cromwell and, more particularly, Anne Boleyn, the woman under whose influence the King had fallen at the time the suggestion about canvassing the universities was made. It is no matter of conjecture that Cranmer went to live in the Boleyns' London mansion for a while, and he must have grown very much in their favor to be asked to accompany the elder Boleyn when he went on his fruitless embassy to Emperor and Pope. However much Cromwell's shrewd intelligence was relied on, Anne may have had more to do with the matter than anybody else when the priest, who was nothing more than the Archdeacon of Taunton, was hurriedly summoned to London upon the death of the aged Archbishop of Canterbury. We need not believe that Cranmer entirely owed his own appointment as Archbishop to Anne Boleyn, but at least he owed a good deal to her patronage, and thus was deeply in her debt. This fact must be always borne in mind with regard to what occurred in 1536.

But Cranmer had soon learned what kind of a man Cromwell was. The power exercised after 1535 by the King's

Vicar-general was forcibly brought home to him when he discovered that Cromwell was not only the greatest figure in politics but even (by delegation) in ecclesiastical affairs. And though Cranmer meddled in politics as little as possible, the ecclesiastical control must have been irksome even to one so mild as himself. He also found reasons for fearing this ruthless and highly efficient man who maintained a kind of private spy system at his own expense. When Mrs. Cranmer came over from Nuremberg, we may be sure Cromwell found out that this quite illegal wife was lurking in the background at Lambeth Palace, and it must have been because of her that the Archbishop paid Cromwell £40 a year. Though the word "blackmail" would probably be too strong, this annual pension to Cromwell—which may have been voluntary—was considered advisable. There were no crimes for which the cautious and correct Archbishop could have been denounced to the King, for though some years later Cranmer began to dabble in novelties which were regarded by rigidly orthodox people as tending towards heresy, Cromwell was himself more deeply implicated, and so was hardly in a position to speak. Whatever Cranmer's reason, it does look as though that £40 a year had something to do with Margaret of Nuremberg.

Cromwell could hardly have had any other handle against Cranmer, and Cranmer may have been aware of facts that were not at all creditable to Cromwell, though, so far as we know, there was no stain upon that formidable man's private life. But since Henry VIII had been well aware of what had been said of Cromwell, even in Wolsey's time, nothing particularly new could have been related, even had Cranmer possessed the hardihood to challenge him. A practical man accepted venality as a matter of course, so long as it was practiced with a show of decorum and was not at the expense of the King himself. It might even be said that a man's willingness to soil his hands in the service of the Crown made him all the more useful. Instead of starting a quarrel with Cromwell, Cranmer found it safer—especially a few years later—to enter a kind of alliance with him.

Obviously nobody was better fitted than Cromwell to be the "hammer of the monks"; as such, he was, in fact, indispensable. But he also acted as the King's First Minister, and if in this respect he was inferior to Wolsey—after all, one of the greatest statesmen Europe has seen—he seemed to be adequate. By working in conjunction with the much better trained Stephen Gardiner, he provided reasonably good service for fairly quiet times. This was especially true after the death of Katharine of Aragon, early in 1536, removed the main cause of friction between Henry VIII and the Emperor Charles V.

Nevertheless disagreements between the King and Cromwell did arise every now and then. Henry did not have much respect for Cromwell, and after one royal rage of more than usual violence Cromwell found it prudent to keep to his house in a diplomatic illness. This time, Cromwell even thought it was not safe to wait, as usual, for the King's anger to cool. He felt that his whole position might be in danger and so used his temporary retirement to devise a means of regaining favor by performing some signal service.

This means he found. Some months before the upheaval he divined what had set Henry's nerves so much on edge. Others had also divined as much, for Chapuys, with whom Cromwell had formed a queer kind of friendship, once when the two men were out hunting together—and were out of earshot—had sounded the First Minister upon the King's getting rid of Anne Boleyn, of whom many knew Henry had grown sick and tired. That time Cromwell returned a laconic, "Not yet," which at least was no suggestion of horror, but since then the situation had changed, and Cromwell was able to think of a means for doing what he knew the King now positively wanted.

On February 7, 1536, Katharine of Aragon, virtually a prisoner at Kimbolton, had died. Upon the arrival of the news, Anne Boleyn, who was clever in a shallow kind of way but not very intelligent, openly rejoiced, thinking this would serve to secure her position. And her position would have become unassailable had she now borne the King a Prince, of which she was in high hopes, as she was well advanced in pregnancy. Had Anne produced a son, Henry would probably have gone down in history as a man who had divorced one wife to marry a second. For he would then have felt obliged to treat Anne with a show of respect, however much philandering he may have done, and he was never very notorious in that capacity. People would not think of him now as a "bluebeard" (actually his beard was of a reddish hue) who sent one wife after another to the block. (Some people, incidentally, have to think hard to remember whether it was Henry VI—perhaps a saint, perhaps a simpleton—who had eight wives or Henry VIII who had six.) But while most of that story does not need retelling here, a discussion of the relations between Anne Boleyn and Thomas Cranmer is inescapable.

Virtually no historian now believes that Anne was guilty of the charges brought against her. Scheming and grasping, yes; vain and frivolous, yes; shrill and shrewish and, in the end, exceedingly tiresome, yes; but a "bad" woman, definitely not. Even the most wanton of women would not have been promiscuous with half a dozen men at the same time, for, quite apart from her husband's disgusted indignation, she would have created jealousies among her lovers. Furthermore, outside of a bawdy-house, she would not herself have undertaken the soliciting of these men—and even within one, such conduct, would, I understand, be contrary to the rules of the game. Nothing said about Anne—and believed at the time and for a long while afterwards—fits in with the character of any ordinary woman, let alone this woman's character.

The suggestion has been made that Anne took a lover— or rather a number of lovers simultaneously—because she had come to believe that Henry could not beget a viable male child. Why on earth should she have had such an idea? If the child which she miscarried within a month of Katharine of Aragon's death was a male, nobody had any means of foretelling its sex, and the royal physicians had no reason to think there was any danger of miscarriage, and finally, the King had no reason to suppose that this child was not his own. The miscarriage was a mere accident, but by the savagely superstitious Henry this was taken as a sign (and he was looking for something to use against a woman he had now come to detest) that his second marriage lay under the same doom as his first. He applied to it the text in Leviticus: "They shall be childless," Anne's daughter Elizabeth not being considered to count, any more than Katharine's daughter Mary (now a young woman of twenty) had been allowed to count. If Anne had miscarried a female child, Henry could hardly have taken this view. But the child would have been a male; as Anne had miscarried of a male, it was a fact that he could pitilessly use against her.

The King had been looking around for some time for a means of ridding himself of Anne. Now he had obtained the means, and in Cromwell he had available a man who knew just how to make use of the means. The first minister dug up evidence (of a kind) that Anne had been adulterous in a wholesale way, using scraps of the indiscreet talk of a woman who had always been unguarded with her tongue.

We need not reproduce this evidence (such as it was), but it could not have carried weight except with a man like Henry VIII, and the carefully packed court that was to hand down the judgment expected of them. One of those accused, a court musician named Mark Smeaton, made some admissions under torture, but the fact that they were extracted under torture where, as Shakespeare was to remark, "men speak anything," made them of no value. In any case, it was on the face of it most unlikely that the Queen would have had any dealings with Smeaton, except perhaps to compliment his skill with the lute. But as he was a soft and gentle creature he might say something damaging, where the others, being of the gentry, with their pride of blood and hardened moreover by their use of weapons in the tilting ring, would have been disdainful in their denials.

Another point comes in: one of those accused was Anne's own brother, Viscount Rochford. The accusation against him was the flimsiest of all: he had been alone with his sister, the Queen, for several hours! Yet the fact sent him to the block, as it sent the others. The only one released of those arrested was Sir Thomas Wyatt, the poet. When he and Anne had been very young there had been a *tendresse* between them. But one of Wyatt's sonnets, which we still have, tells her that he is going to sheer off, she being made to remark in it, "Caesar's I am." It may be suspected that it was not this that saved him but Cromwell's instinctive perception that it would be unwise to make the whole story incredible: surely five lovers would serve his purpose as well as (or better than) the six with whom he started.

For a King to chop off the head of his Queen is undeniably shocking. Yet one constantly reads in the papers of an outraged husband shooting his wife, or her paramour, or both. However, what is called in France a *crime passionelle* is often leniently dealt with, and even in some parts of the United States the "unwritten law" has frequently been successfully invoked. But though Henry VIII could not say he had acted in blind fury, we must grant that if a Queen-consort takes a lover, she can be held guilty of treason, for any child adulterously conceived might supplant the real heir to the throne, and her lover could be guilty of treason for the same reason.

Furthermore, since only official reports were circulated, with no publication of evidence that anybody could study in the newspapers, the guilt of Anne and her five supposititious lovers was generally accepted as proved. We find that even Queen Mary at the end of her life brought herself to believe that Mark Smeaton and not the King was the real father of the future Elizabeth I. This, however, counts for little: the views Mary expressed coincided with her prejudices, for she was rightly doubtful of the sincerity of Elizabeth's protestations of Catholicism. It is doubtful whether she herself ever set eyes on Mark Smeaton, so she must have been merely repeating what somebody else had said.

However, the opinion prevalent at the time of Anne's

97

downfall must be allowed for, though of course its prevalence does not make it sound. Coolly examined, one must dismiss the whole thing as preposterous, for while it may be conceivable that Queen Anne had taken a lover in lonely desperation, there is nothing to justify such a belief. The reason she fell was that Henry was sick to death of her, and was looking for a pretext to act as he did.

Cromwell undoubtedly fabricated the whole affair, by way of ingratiating himself with the King. It was not at all difficult to do so, as Anne had always been loose of tongue, so loose that Lord Rochford had at least once found it necessary to warn her to be more guarded. Very likely she did sometimes criticize the King's clothes, which were, indeed, over-opulent. But if she criticized his poetry (which was also charged against her at her trial), it must be said that for this she did not have the slightest qualification. Some of Henry's poetry was first-rate, and of his music some is still performed by chamber orchestras, as one or two of his hymns are still sung in English cathedrals.* In any event, criticism of this sort had nothing to do with the offense for which she was being tried, unless it was adduced as further proof that she had ceased to love him. The truth is that she was being tried because, after being infatuated with her, he had grown to loathe her.

Now for Thomas Cranmer's connection with Anne Boleyn's fall. He had in no way brought it about. Rather he was seriously alarmed at her arrest—and on such a charge —and a good many people who knew that she had promoted his fortunes would not have been surprised if he had fallen too. Cromwell, with cold and ruthless cynicism, worked upon

* Some of his poetry has probably been lost; this is certainly the case with the Mass we know that he composed.

the consternation which he, quite correctly, guessed that the Archbishop felt. There could hardly have been any serious intention of harming the poor man, but the fears could be used against Anne, and might also serve as a cracking of the whip over Cranmer, a further notice that he had better do exactly as he was told.

Anne was arrested on May Day, 1536, and her lovers at the same time (except for Smeaton who had been arrested a day or two in advance), quite secretly, so that the blow would fall on the others with devastating suddenness. On May third, from Lambeth Palace, Cranmer wrote a letter to the King, from which a few sentences might be quoted or summarized.* So far from the letter being a defense of the unfortunate woman to whom he owed a good deal, it takes back with one hand everything (and more) that he has given with the other. Cranmer lets the King know that he has been summoned to Lambeth and is writing at his command, which incidentally told him that he was not to go into the royal presence without express permission—something which sounded ominous.

The Archbishop begins by urging the King "somewhat to suppress the great sorrow of your Grace's heart, and to take all adversities of God's hands both patiently and thankfully." The Archbishop was not aware that Henry was already thankful all right, though Cromwell was well aware of this. The latter not only knew of Henry's wish to get

---

* I am quoting from the text as given in the *Miscellaneous Writings and Letters of Thomas Cranmer,* edited by John Edmund Cox for the Parker Society in 1846, pp. 323–24. It is also included in one of the five volumes of English Prose, edited in 1922 by W. Peacock for the "World's Classics." No doubt it is also included in the *Letters and Papers, Henry VIII,* but as they are exceedingly voluminous I have not paused to look it up there.

rid of Anne Boleyn (Cranmer may have vaguely known that the royal marriage was foundering), but he had been one of those entertained by Sir William Seymour at Wolf Hall at Severnake. There Henry had already settled in his own mind that Sir William's blonde, commonplace daughter was to be his third wife. Indeed, while Queen Anne was in the Tower, the King was—as all London knew—making Jane Seymour nightly visits in his barge, all lit up and with a band playing. As Chapuys acidly remarked, he had never known a man who "took his horns more pleasantly."

Jane was a circumspect young woman—and not so very young—for under the coaching of her brother Edward, the future Protector of Edward VI's time, she returned a purse of gold the King gave her, saying that she could not accept this except as a dowry when she married. Henry was enchanted by such demure virtue, which probably *was* virtue. As Jane, when very young, had been a lady-in-waiting to Katharine of Aragon, she was one of that Queen's adherents. This meant that she never regarded Anne as Henry's wife or considered that she was supplanting her. But if Jane was quiet and modest and not aggressively ambitious, her scheming brothers made up for everything; they intended to make use of Jane for their own advancement.

But to continue with Cranmer's letter of May 3rd to the King: "I cannot but deny that your Grace hath great causes many ways of lamentable heaviness; and also, that in the wrongful estimation of the world your Grace's honor is so highly touched (whether the things that be commonly spoken be true, or not) that I remember not that ever Almighty God sent unto your Grace any like occasion to try your Grace's constancy throughout, whether your Grace can be content to take of God's hand as well things displeasant as pleasant." He adds some more praise of Henry's virtues and then goes on: "If it be true that is openly reported of the Queen's Grace; if men had a right estimation of things, they should not esteem any part of your Grace's honor to be touched. . . . And my mind is clean amazed; for I never had better opinion in women; which maketh me to think, that she be not culpable. And again, I think your Highness would not have gone so far with her, except she surely had been culpable. . . . And if she be found culpable, considering your Grace's goodness towards her, and from what condition your Grace of your mere goodness took her and set the crown upon her head; I repute him not your Grace's faithful servant and subject, nor true unto the realm, that would not desire the offence without mercy to be punished to the example of all other. And as I loved her not a little for the love which I judged her to bear towards God and His Gospel; so, if she be proved culpable, there is not one that loveth God and His Gospel that ever will favor her, but must hate her above all other; and the more they favor the Gospel, the more they will hate her; for then there was never creature in our time that so much slandered the Gospel; and God hath sent her this punishment, for that she feignedly hath professed his Gospel in her mouth, but not in heart and deed."

There is more, but that will surely be enough, except the bit where Cranmer tells the King, "Your Grace's favor to the Gospel was led not by affection unto her, but by zeal unto the truth." He does, however, draw the line at saying that the King married her, not because he loved her (or lusted after her) but because of her religious views. To have said that would of course have been monstrously ludicrous; even what he did say is hardly true, for the Boleyn

101

family had only made professions that suited Henry, though Anne herself seems to have developed more piety than we can discover in her father and brother, no doubt because of her close contact with the devout Henry.

Regarding this letter many comments have been made. First I will make my own. One would hardly gather from it that the writer was one of the greatest masters of English prose. This could be accounted for on the ground of Cranmer's agitation at the time; but the same thing can be said of his "official" letters and his wordy and windy controversial works, all of which are at least three times as long as they need be. They do, however, manage to convey his meaning, which is a considerable literary virtue. Belloc somewhat maliciously says of the earlier letter in which Cranmer "asked" permission to try the royal divorce case that it is all a single sentence—the longest in English literature. I could produce even longer sentences from the sermons of John Donne, and they are as magnificent prose as one would wish to find. (The clipped style of Hemingway, in his first phase, may be good, but surely not so good as Donne's.) The other comment to which I might draw attention is one in which Dame Edith Sitwell describes this letter as very "brave." Since then (and quite recently) she has become a Catholic, a brave action on her part. But really, religious views do not enter into the matter: let the reader judge for himself whether Cranmer was brave. Personally I am ready with an extenuation: everybody believed Anne guilty, and Cranmer was doing what he could; had he been more cowed he would have said nothing.

But the letter just quoted has a postscript, one written after Cranmer had been summoned to the Star-Chamber. It does not add much except to say, "I am exceedingly sorry that such faults can be proved by [against] the Queen, as I heard by their relation." Apparently the principle had not yet been established that anybody charged with any sort of crime is regarded as innocent until proved guilty. In the main body of his letter to the King Cranmer did every once in a while express the hope that Anne was not "culpable"; all such hope was dropped after what he had been told in the Star-Chamber: he accepted the fact that Anne was guilty, though she had not yet been tried.

After her trial, in which Anne defended herself in a spirited kind of way, and with some adroitness (though the verdict was predetermined) Cromwell was brought in again in a new capacity. The King was determined by now that Elizabeth should be put out of the line of succession—not merely to spite Anne but also because of a not unreasonable suspicion that the supposititious adulteries had been going on for a long time, and that Elizabeth was not his own child. Therefore an annulment of his marriage to Anne had to be obtained. Cranmer was sent to her to extract the necessary confessions. The first idea was that she had never been married to Henry because she had made a precontract with the young man who was now the Earl of Northumberland. Apparently Anne might have admitted this—as Cranmer went to her empowered to say that she would be free to go to Antwerp, a promise which he no doubt gave in good faith, put up to offering it by the King or Cromwell, or both. But Northumberland, though he was most unhappily married to a daughter of the Earl of Shrewsbury, absolutely denied the precontract; though not a very strong character, he had a sense of honor, and he took an oath on the Blessed Sacrament. Therefore that way of escape was blocked.

Upon what grounds the annulment was obtained was

never published. But Chapuys, a man very much in the know, wrote Charles V the reason was that Henry, previous to his marriage to Anne, had had her sister Mary Boleyn as his mistress, thus creating the impediment of incest. For this Clement VII, in Cardinal Wolsey's days, had given a dispensation—conditional upon Henry's getting a Papal decree of annulment of his marriage to Katharine of Aragon. But now Cranmer was able to take the line that no Papal dispensation was of any value in England. However, to have given this out officially was impossible, or at least inadvisable. But nobody, so far as I am aware, has suggested any other grounds for annulment as possible. Chapuys was undoubtedly right in what he wrote to the Emperor.

One can imagine the scene between Cranmer, the gentle wheedler of women, and the special friend of this woman, whom he would have liked to help. But it is necessary to refrain from imagining such a scene, unless one aims at fiction, though fiction often reveals more truth than historical documents. All that need be said is that Parliament eventually bastardized poor little Elizabeth, just as Mary had been bastardized. All was perfectly logical, but it left Henry VIII in a worse case than ever, with no legitimate heir to the throne, though he still was toying with the fantastic notion of declaring his one bastard son, the Duke of Richmond, his heir by will. He had thought of this long before, and may have been deterred only by the certainty that a civil war would have resulted. Young Fitzroy, now seventeen, was sent to be one of the witnesses of Anne's execution, but as he died shortly afterwards, the danger of his being proclaimed King in succession to Henry was luckily removed.

All this did not weigh heavily upon the King. He intended to marry Jane Seymour, with the shortest possible delay. Anne was beheaded on May nineteenth; the next day he was betrothed to Jane, and ten days later he married her—probably not because he was madly in love with her but because he counted upon her to produce a legitimate child. When this proved to be a son he was not only overjoyed but felt himself completely justified in the way he had freed himself from marriage from his two previous wives, each union being pronounced incestuous.

The sentence given Anne was that she might be either burned or beheaded, according to the King's will. If the burning sounds barbarous—as, indeed, it was—it conformed with a law which was on the statute book and was occasionally enforced even in the late eighteenth century. But Henry, so far from enforcing it in all its rigor, permitted Anne, as she had a great dread of the axe, to have her head cut off by the expert swordsman from Calais, specially summoned for the purpose. Sir William Kingston, the Constable of the Tower, assured her that she would feel no pain whatever, as the stroke would be "so subtle." The four gentlemen lovers laid their heads on the block; but Mark Smeaton was sent to die at Tyburn.

Lord Rochford's condemnation was, like those of the others accused, a foregone conclusion. But even had it not been so, he made it certain by an act that he did to revenge himself upon Henry. When handed up a question in writing, because the prosecution did not wish it to be heard, he haughtily read it aloud in the courtroom. It asked whether the Queen had ever told him that the King was impotent. Of course men of forty-seven (and Henry was prematurely old) often lose their potency, as do even younger men, and it is more than likely that the King's sexual powers had diminished considerably. But that he was *not* impotent, and could even beget a son, is proved by the birth the following year of Edward VI. In any event it is unlikely (though not impossible) that Anne had discussed this matter with her brother. Even had she done so, one cannot see how such a discussion would have been treasonable. But Henry VIII was absurdly vain of his virility, and very sensitive about the matter at a moment when he meant to marry again very soon. Rochford's reading the question aloud was sufficient to doom him.

Anne Boleyn was given the same apartments in the Tower which she had occupied three years before on the night prior to her coronation. Her conduct there was really astonishing but probably can be explained on the ground of hysteria: she vacillated rapidly between terror and levity, but of course hers had always been a shallow character, except for a resolute determination to obtain her own ends. However, after a while she calmed down—and she gained several days' delay in waiting for the Calais swordsman. And she asked that the Blessed Sacrament be exposed in a little oratory adjoining her room, and there she spent much time in prayer. When the hour came for her to go to the scaffold, she died with dignity, protesting her innocence with her last breath.

The other duty Cranmer was called upon to perform was to issue a dispensation for Henry and Jane Seymour to marry —but it was a routine matter. As Jane was very remotely of royal descent, according to the strict ideas of that time, there was consanguinity. A stroke of the pen sufficed for so simple, so hypothetical, a matter.

Chapter Ten

The Heretic Hounds
the Heretics

Strictly speaking, Thomas Cranmer may have inclined towards heresy at the time he became Archbishop of Canterbury in 1533, but he was not really a heretic. His theology imperceptively varied from that of the majority of Englishmen, being Catholic, except for his rejection of the Pope's Supremacy. But he was soon regarded as an "advanced" man, though this was not so much on account of definitely formulated opinions as because he came to identify himself with those considered tinged by what was called the "New Learning." But it would be a serious injustice to think of him as one secretly working against the orthodox Faith, and making hypocritical pretenses which he carefully concealed so long as Henry VIII lived and then promptly dropped the moment the old King died.

This is not to affirm that his beliefs before 1547 did not gradually develop in what we should now call a Protestant direction, for it is virtually certain that they did, although he found it prudent not to say too much about them. More and more he worked in close co-operation with Thomas Cromwell—except in relation to the expropriation of monasteries, for that was a work Cromwell reserved to himself, and one with which Cranmer was glad he had nothing to do—yet where Cromwell in his last moments at Tyburn publicly repudiated the errors he had so largely fomented, he seemed during the years when he was all-powerful to have no concern except for public policy or his private profit, whereas Cranmer was a sincerely religious man, though perhaps not a notably pious one. Yet in the marching-song of the Pilgrimage of Grace his name was joined to those of Cromwell and Sir Richard Rich as the three men the Pilgrims demanded the King should dismiss. For though Rich was the head of the Court of Augmentation set up to deal with the spoils of the monasteries, and Cranmer had had nothing to do with that matter, he was still not forgiven by the country for the part he had taken in the royal divorce. What he had done in the Anne Boleyn affair was kept dark, but had it been known, the English people would have believed that she got only her just deserts and not have given Cranmer any credit, as now we find it necessary, on the contrary, to find excuses for him.

When Robert Aske, the leader of the Pilgrimage of Grace, came up to London to see the King and was so affably received that he returned to Yorkshire in the belief that all the Pilgrims' demands were to be granted—never guessing what butchery was soon to follow the broken promise, or that he himself would be hanged in chains—Cromwell found it advisable to retire, for the time being, into the shadows, while the gentle and courteous Cranmer was brought forward. But the policy of betrayal did not emanate from the Archbishop (no policy did, not even, except in a limited way, ecclesiastical policy). Cranmer was merely a man who seemed very mild and harmless; it was Henry himself who supplied the charm, as it was he and Cromwell and the Duke of Norfolk who devised the scheme of perfidy.

The rising known as the Pilgrimage of Grace (it is more accurate to describe it as a protest), though it presented some economic grievances, was mainly prompted by the expropriation of the smaller monasteries under the act of 1536. It is conclusive proof that the monasteries were popular, and incidentally shows that people in their locality—those who were best acquainted with them—knew that they were not corrupt. The King, under the advice of Cromwell, made the Pilgrimage of Grace a pretext for taking over the larger monasteries, though these had been highly commended by Parliament for their virtue and good discipline in 1536. The argument was that they must have given some aid and comfort to the Pilgrims (which may possibly have been true in a few cases). Gradually, under pressure or threats—usually actively applied persuasion sufficed—every one of them was surrendered to the King by 1540.

This looting, though it was for the benefit of the Crown —a large part of the plunder always going to the newly rich who sanctioned it—was something which Cranmer, and all far-sighted and kindly men, had to regard with some misgiving. Such men were of course quite out of sympathy with rapacity which, indeed, greatly increased under King Edward VI, with Cranmer then making some protest, such as he never dared to make in Henry's time. But the Archbishop of Canterbury was a somewhat ineffectual person, partly because he was not at all aggressive but always agreeable in manner and sometimes rather timid. He may not emerge with much glory, yet little, if any, of the disgrace of that period became attached to him.

The Pilgrimage of Grace had been a fiasco. Yet Henry knew that 30,000 Pilgrims had assembled at Doncaster, and that they could have been very dangerous had they struck.

So while he would not deviate from his general policy, the Bluff King Hal—a man absurdly scared of any rumor of pestilence and who in his several wars never led any troops into battle, thinking it enough to prance about in armor on a horse—did something to placate his subjects. This was his preparation of the *Institution of a Christian Man,* upon the whole a Catholic statement of doctrine, inadequate though it is, to which Cranmer was one of the bishops who contributed chapters. It almost seemed, in fact, to represent a Catholic reaction that went on until there appeared, in 1539, the Act of Six Articles, or the Whip of Six Strings. *That* was in several ways more Catholic than the Pope, for it asserted that the celibacy of the clergy was a part of the divine law instead of being, what it really is, merely a disciplinary regulation. Also, it made the denial of Transubstantiation punishable by burning, without providing any means of recantation.

This act, however, was too drastic to be enforced, except in a spasmodic fashion. Cranmer, naturally alarmed, is said to have hurriedly sent Mrs. Cranmer back to Germany. If she ever came back during Henry's reign, he was more than ever careful to keep her out of sight. As for the burnings, not a great many occurred, except in 1540, for the King was disposed to be negligent. One cannot but suspect—and this is rather more than suspicion—that Cranmer and Cromwell co-operated in the virtual nullification of the Act; when victims had to be found they could always lay by the heels the refugees from the continent, loosely called Anabaptists, though they were of various heretical opinion.

The question of persecutions for heresy during Henry's reign, however, demands some qualification. For instance, in 1533 John Frith was burned (and he was by no means the only one at that time), and such burnings went on sporadically until 1545, when Anne Askew suffered. Cranmer had some share in both condemnations. On the Frith commission he sat as a member along with Thomas Boleyn—Viscount Rochford as he was then—which shows that Cranmer held the ordinary views about persecution. It also shows that the Boleyns were not quite correctly described by Chapuys as "more Lutheran than Luther himself." We may perhaps say that the Boleyns were self-seeking politicians of no very definite religious opinions. Neither thing can be said of Cranmer. We might merely remember that he was anything but opposed to the burning of heretics, even at the time when he himself was burned.

Cranmer was upon the whole a moderate man, especially at this stage in his career; but one never knew when Henry VIII would have a sudden flare-up of piety and exhibit it in the ordinary way by burning somebody. Calvin burned Servetus in 1553 for his Unitarian principles, and some of those who suffered under Queen Mary (including Cranmer himself) accepted and applied the standards of the time and so had no grounds for complaint on that score. Cranmer had to take his part in persecution, especially as he was Archbishop of Canterbury, but his heart was never in business of this kind, no matter how fully his head accepted the concept that heretics deserved the stake. Though in the light of his own subsequent heresy, he has sometimes been accused of vile hypocrisy in sending others to the stake for what he held himself, the worst that can be justly said of him is that he was perhaps too much given to mouthing what passed for piety. His religion, while sincere, was not a blazing conviction but had about it too much routine and formalism. It is a shortcoming with which half of our so-called Christians can be charged, so it is hardly fair to stress this in the case of Cranmer. He did, indeed, eventually become very much of a heretic; he was orthodox enough at this time.

What may be added is that—largely as a part of Cromwell's foreign policy—during the end of the seventh lustrum of the sixteenth century Henry was induced to seek allies among the German princes, and that Cranmer then took an active part in the meetings held in London with some Lutheran theologians. This was natural enough: as Archbishop of Canterbury he was the proper person to preside at the conferences. Moreover, he knew German fairly well, whereas the foreign languages that Englishmen of his time knew were French (and this most often) and perhaps Italian and Spanish. If Cranmer himself held any novel theological ideas he was too prudent to parade them, and the gatherings broke down because the King himself would not hear the demands being made by the Lutherans for Communion in both kinds, permission for priests to marry, and the abolition of private Masses. Left to himself, Cranmer might have been willing to compromise but would have been in the minority among the English bishops. At any rate nothing came of the project.

But in one important matter Cranmer—or rather Cromwell, using Cranmer as a shield behind which he could operate—hoodwinked the King, and that is in securing the publication of an authorized vernacular Bible. We must remember that there was no objection to an English translation of the Scriptures—as a general matter—but only to a particular version. Never must we imagine that Wycliffe's translation—circulated only in manuscript and, for that reason, only in sections—was the first translation to appear. Sir Thomas More wrote that he had often seen English translations of the Bible in the hands of good Catholics, translations allowed them by their bishops, though again one would infer that usually these were merely sections of the Bible. When Tyndale brought out his translation, which was largely based upon Luther's and in many places was very inaccurate, his version was prohibited, such copies as were smuggled into England being confiscated and burned.

The prohibition, however, was not against *any* translation of the Bible into English, but merely one which was heretical, and it could be made heretical by the appended notes as well as by falsification of key words in the text. Even so, it may be granted that Tyndale and his collaborator, Coverdale, laid the foundation of what finally emerged, for they (and especially Tyndale) had great literary gifts. But Henry VIII would not sanction this version under any circumstances, ostensibly because of the heresy it contained, but also because Tyndale opposed Henry's divorce of Katharine of Aragon.

Tyndale's errors were removed, with few exceptions, by the Authorized Version made during the reign of James I, and by still earlier translators. But all of them, including the group of Catholics who produced the Douay-Rheims version, are in Tyndale's debt to this extent: he provided what may be described as the basic "tone" of the Bible in English. But though Tyndale should not be undervalued—despite his errors—Henry was determined that this version should not be sanctioned, for which reason Cromwell, aided by Cranmer, introduced it by playing a trick upon the King.

To introduce Tyndale under his own name was, of course, out of the question, so John Rogers, one of those whom Queen Mary sent to the stake, gave the Tyndale translation a kind of sponsorship. Yet as Rogers was himself suspected of heresy, his name was also kept off the title-page. That of an entirely fictitious "Thomas Matthew" was used instead. This translation was printed in Paris and, because of its size, was called the "Great" Bible. Expensive as it was, every English parish church was obliged to purchase one or more copies.

This version appeared in England in 1539, and Cranmer wrote a preface for the reprintings of 1540 and 1541. Though the Lutheran notes were suppressed, there were complaints of inaccuracies in the text itself, and Henry ordered that it be revised, the task being assigned to the English universities, with the result that no revision was ever completed. But by this time the authority of the Bible had begun to be pitted against the doctrines of the Church—especially by men of defective education—and a great deal of harm was done. This may be why some Catholics to this day are rather suspicious of vernacular renderings, although a good many translations have been produced by unimpeachably orthodox scholars. Still, this may not be the whole explanation: while the Church encourages the reading of the Bible (even giving an indulgence to its readers), never is the Bible to be considered as more than *one* of the sources of the Church's authority. Even the best of renderings may be dangerous to people unless they place their main reliance upon the *Ecclesia docens*.

During Henry VIII's reign, Thomas Cranmer, as Archbishop of Canterbury, had to play his part in upholding orthodoxy, as was also true when Edward VI was on the throne, though by then the concept of what was orthodox had changed in many respects, and largely because Cranmer's own ideas had changed. In Henry's reign he had a share in the spectacular show staged by the King himself when, in 1539, a man named John Lambert (alias Nicholson) was brought before him on a charge of having denied the Real Presence. The King presided, and this bishop or that, in turn (Cranmer was one of them), was called upon to refute the errors of the accused.* Stephen Gardiner in later years expressed dissatisfaction with the way Cranmer did so, but this was said in the light of Cranmer's subsequent development. At the time he was sufficiently orthodox. At any rate Lambert (or Nicholson) was duly burned at the stake, the sentence being read out, on behalf of the King, by Cromwell.

The Act of the Six Articles was passed by Parliament the following year. This act seemed to Cranmer to go too far (as it certainly did) and the Archbishop made some written comments upon its more stringent items, cautiously venturing to disagree occasionally with the King. How cautious the disagreement was comes out in the famous sentence: "This is my judgment at present, which, however, I do not temerariously maintain, referring all to your Majesty." Henry liked a man whose disagreements were so mildly expressed. Gardiner was disposed to be blunter; so was Cromwell, though he every now and then got a royal pummeling, as Henry, even while finding him useful, did not hold him in much respect. As a matter of fact, Henry vastly enjoyed a theological argument, which could hardly be carried on

* At Cranmer's trial at Oxford in September, 1555, he was bluntly asked by Dr. Martin, one of his prosecutors: "What doctrine taught you when you condemned Lambert the sacramentary, in the King's presence at Whitehall?" And Cranmer answered, "I maintained then the papists' doctrine." It might be added that it was Henry VIII and not Cranmer who condemned Nicholson, but Cranmer was called upon to refute the man. (*Miscellaneous Writings and Letters of Thomas Cranmer*, the Parker Society, 1846, p. 218.)

with a man who assented to everything; but his opponents were well advised in the end to admit that the King had beaten down all opposition and had convinced them that they had been holding an untenable position.

Cromwell, having failed to bring off his earlier scheme for a rapprochement with the German Protestant princes, tried again from a new angle. When Henry was in the marriage market again after the death of Jane Seymour, Cromwell had the idea that, if he took Anne, the sister of the Duke of Cleves, as his new wife, the German princes would be won over. The Duke of Cleves was not professedly a Lutheran, though he inclined in that direction, and he might be used to soften up men of stronger Lutheran convictions than his own. At least he was a German and, as such, might help to draw the princes to Henry's side, against the Emperor.

Holbein was commissioned to paint the lady's portrait, and was instructed that it would be as well to make her seem a bit handsomer than she really was. Yet judging from the portrait, which still exists, Holbein must have found that he could not do much with her. Whatever his instructions may have been, his art was of the realistic, almost the "photographic" sort, and he could not change what was more important to him than a large fee from an English patron. While he may have "improved" Anne's looks slightly, she still stands before us as a buxom German *hausfrau*. In fact one is inclined to say that of all of Henry VIII's six wives —the best favored of whom was probably Katharine of Aragon in her youth, though even she was not a beauty but had only the freshness of youth and an open, innocent face —Anne of Cleves was the least prepossessing. The taste of the times should be allowed for, so should the way people dressed; but some of the portraits that have come down to us from the sixteenth century are of women who in any age would seem attractive, and rather more than that. Henry does not appear to have been any connoisseur of feminine pulchritude, but in the case of Anne of Cleves one is obliged to do some wondering. After all, he did have the Holbein painting of her before he saw her, and it impressed him. We must conclude that his dismay after their actual meeting sprang from something other than that she was no "Miss Universe."

In some ways he should have been more than satisfied, for when he was thinking, shortly before this, of marrying one of the French King's relatives, he let Francis I know that, as he was a large man (which was putting it mildly) he thought a tall and brawny wife would suit him best. Well, in Anne of Cleves he got precisely that—not a fat woman but one of more than average height and sturdily built. One cannot believe that he found the lady physically repulsive, but undoubtedly he thought her dull. She could speak no English, or, indeed, any language except German, so she and her husband could not talk to one another. Besides she knew no games, nor could she sing (strange in a German!) nor even, one surmises, put that gawky frame of hers through a dance, simple as most of the dances of the time were. She was, however, very good-natured, and that must have counted for something, but the voracious way she gobbled down her food and drank vast quantities of beer was just a bit too much even for such a trencherman as Henry.

All this might have been put up with, and the King would probably have come to find Anne agreeable enough in time, had it not been for one thing: the marriage in a very short time was seen to be a liability rather than an asset. Henry had gone into it expecting that he would be strengthened by a coalition of German princes, not because he was planning to make war upon the Emperor but just in case the Emperor had a dispute (he did not look for Charles to declare war) with him. Instead Charles threatened war with the Duke of Cleves, and, according to the terms of the marriage contract, Henry was bound to go to the Duke's aid against Charles—about the very last thing he wanted to do. He therefore cast around in his mind for some means to rid himself of the Duke's sister at once. Cromwell had seriously blundered in his foreign policy, and the easiest way of rectifying the matter was for Henry to divorce Anne of Cleves. As there was no charge of misconduct that could possibly be brought against her, Henry was obliged to make out that he had found her so distasteful that the marriage had never been consummated, which meant that, though a marriage ceremony had been performed, there had been no real marriage.

Cromwell had been highly efficient in uprooting the monks, and this had greatly enriched the King (although he had found it necessary to share the spoils with the powerful people in the country). One might have expected Henry to be grateful for this signal service, but gratitude was not part of his nature. The nobles who had been enriched in the process were now all the more powerful, and as they had always been resentful that the upstart Cromwell had made himself a kind of dictator, they now saw their chance to ruin him. They, like the King, had utilized him, but now that all the monasteries had gone, there was no further need of Cromwell.

Henry VIII could strike very savagely and suddenly, as

often as not when the blow was least expected. However, the fact that he made Cromwell Earl of Essex just after the Cleves marriage was probably not a way of masking his dissatisfaction with Anne (or of Cromwell who had negotiated the marriage) but rather a reward for the alliance he had brought about. No doubt the King was never exactly delighted with his new wife, but one must suspect that the disgust with her that he came to express so loudly, was intensified when he found that the political advantages he thought he would gain were actually disadvantages. In the interval, Cromwell retained unimpaired authority, while the Duke of Norfolk and other members of the old nobility were quietly sharpening their knives to cut his throat, of course with Henry's knowledge and consent.

It seems incredible that Cromwell, with his private spy system, should have had no idea what was going on. If anybody did warn him he must have thought himself unassailable. But there were some signs that he should have considered ominous. An Augustinian ex-Prior named Barnes, a protégé of Cromwell's, had attacked Bishop Gardiner at Paul's Cross and though he was commanded to make a retractation, it was not groveling enough, so into the Tower he went, emerging only to be burned at Smithfield. One cannot but feel that Barnes's having been sent to Cleves had something to do with the matter. As for Gardiner and Cromwell they dined together amicably in March, so it was supposed that they had closed their quarrel and that Cromwell was safe.

It was not so at all. One day, after having attended a session of Parliament in the morning he went in the afternoon to a meeting of the Council. There the Duke, who was presiding, gave a signal and armed guards marched in to ar-

rest Cromwell for treason. Though Cromwell made a fine
show of the indignation that had so often been intimidat-
ing in the past, he was hurried at once by a side exit to a
waiting barge. This took him to his house where clerks
were already making an inventory of his valuables. As indicated in the fine Holbein portrait of him now in the
Frick Collection in New York, he was a notable collector of
objets d'art, of which a good many had been rifled from
the suppressed monasteries. Other clerks were already on
their way to his many manors. The interesting thing is that
when Parliament passed its attainder against him—with no
dissenting voice, though he had packed that Parliament—
Henry, in spite of the fact that everything Cromwell owned
was subject to confiscation by the Crown, permitted Cromwell's son Gregory to keep part of his father's property,
though not his earldom. The explanation must be that
Gregory had married a widowed sister of the Seymours,
which made him almost a brother-in-law to the King.
Gregory was an oafish, sluggish young man, good for nothing, but quite harmless. The mercy tendered him bordered
on contempt.

But no mercy was tendered Thomas Cromwell; everybody hated him. His ability was recognized, but so were his
chicanery and ruthlessness. The only question was whether
he should be beheaded, as befitted a man of title (though
he was stripped of his earldom at once), or hanged at Tyburn
as an ordinary traitor. The compromise was that he should
be beheaded at Tyburn. Henry saw to it, however, that
he was spared for a couple of months, long enough to give
him hope that he was not to be executed after all, for he
ended one of his letters to the King with the cry, "Mercy!
mercy! mercy!" That only made people wonder that one

whom they had supposed was compounded of iron had proved so lacking in common fortitude.

Cranmer was sorry for the fate that had befallen one who had been a friend—after a sort. But while he had collaborated with Cromwell in some of his doings (though not in the plunder of the monks), he had done so because he was well aware that Cromwell held a whip over him which he would not hesitate to use if that ever became necessary. Such being the case it would not have been surprising if Cranmer had rejoiced in Cromwell's fall. It is an indication of the Archbishop's gentle character that he made a plea to the King on behalf of Cromwell. Cranmer's letter was not unlike the "plea" he had made in 1536 on behalf of Anne Boleyn, in that it contained some groveling. But far from his thinking that he could in any way change a policy decided upon, there may be here (as there certainly was when Anne Boleyn fell) some fear that his having worked with Cromwell might be held against him. However, this time he stood in no special danger, for at least he had had nothing to do with the Cleves marriage, though he may have thought privately that an alliance with the German princes might be of some advantage to the King.

However this may be, on June 14, 1540, he wrote Henry a letter which, in part, reads: "I heard yesterday in your Grace's Council that he [Cromwell] is a traitor; yet who cannot be sorrowful and amazed that he should be a traitor against your Majesty . . . he who loved your Majesty (as I thought) no less than God. . . . I loved him as my friend, for so I took him to be; but I chiefly loved him for the love which I thought I saw him bear ever towards your Grace, above all other. But now if he be a traitor, I am sorry that ever I loved or trusted him, and I am very glad that his treason is discovered in time; but yet again I am sorrowful; for whom shall your Grace trust hereafter, if you might not trust him? Alas! I bewail and lament your Grace's chance therein, I wot not whom your Grace may trust." *

Again Cranmer takes the Council's word therein, without the least proof that there had been treason, for though Cromwell had no doubt made an egregious error in policy, his intentions were good in that respect, and the charge that he was planning to lead a rebellion is utterly ridiculous, for a man so detested would have found no followers. He was of course a rascal then, as he had been for close to ten years, and probably a good deal longer, but the King knew that perfectly well, and had found Cromwell all the more useful in consequence. Perhaps Cranmer saw only the best side of a man who did, after all, have a good side. The last sentence quoted can mean only one thing: that the King had better beware of the Duke of Norfolk and Bishop Gardiner, the leaders of a conservative group, who might now be free to head a Catholic reaction. We may accept the letter as a sincere attempt to do something for Cromwell; still more was it an attempt (even more sincere) to do something for Cranmer himself. In any case, Cromwell could be considered as no more than a friend—a somewhat dictatorial one—and perhaps hardly more than a friendly acquaintance. If he had had anything to do with Cranmer's appointment as Archbishop, he had only advised this as good policy. Cranmer cannot be said to have owed to Cromwell a tenth of what he had owed to Anne Boleyn, nor could his letter, written ostensibly to aid Cromwell, seem to have

* Cf. *Miscellaneous Writings and Letters of Thomas Cranmer,* the Parker Society, 1846, p. 401.

done Cromwell any harm, even if it failed to do him any good.

Cromwell was given time to write out what could be used by Henry to obtain a divorce from Anne of Cleves, mainly to exaggerate the disgust Henry said he felt for his German wife so as to make it appear that in consequence the marriage had never been consummated. He used expressions so nasty it is hard to believe Henry could have used them at all. One of the choice bits is that the King told him on the morning after his marriage night: "I have felt her belly and breasts and thereby, as I can judge, she should be no maid, which struck me to the heart when I felt them that I had neither will nor courage to proceed further." I submit that not even the coarsest grained of men talks like that even to his most intimate friend. But it was written evidence, what must be described as an affidavit, and it came in very handy for Henry's purpose. Moreover, with shame one has to say that other courtiers said much the same thing—all of which must be suspected as merely a means of obtaining the royal favor.

That the King had slept a number of nights with his bride was dismissed as immaterial, though, long years before, Cardinals Wolsey and Campeggio had been offered less than this as presumptive proof that young sickly Prince Arthur and Katharine of Aragon had consummated *their* marriage, something that Katharine and her ladies-in-waiting had most emphatically denied at the time—that is, long before the proceedings for annulling her marriage to Henry on these grounds. Nevertheless an obedient Convocation declared the marriage of Henry and Anne of Cleves null and void. Cranmer did not sit in judgment upon the matter, which is to his credit. Nor did he take any leading part in what the Convocation did, the main speech there being made by Stephen Gardiner.

Anne probably could have contested the matter, if only on the grounds of probability. Perhaps she did not know enough English to understand what was happening, or she may have pretended not to understand. By being complaisant she obtained a number of manor houses and what amounted to well over £100,000 a year, if we reckon her endowment in modern money. She was also gracefully retired with the title of the "King's Sister." As Henry visited her every now and then, he could not have found her person so very distasteful. The only condition imposed was that she remain in England, and she herself preferred England to provincial Cleves. Her marriage to Henry is now regarded as rather a good joke.

Chapter Eleven

In Danger

Bully though Cromwell was, he was also something of a protector to Cranmer. Yet Cranmer probably was never in much danger so far as Henry was concerned, nor was any man who did not set himself in determined opposition to the royal will; at other times the King tried, in his own fashion, to be just, and he had so much bonhomie that he was not difficult to manage by those who took reasonable precautions. Cranmer has often been described as merely subservient to the King; a truer statement of the case was that Henry, like nearly everyone else, liked the unpretentious and courteous Archbishop, and that they shared the same *Weltanschauung.*

Nevertheless Cranmer had some enemies. Stephen Gardiner was the one most to be feared, though his animosity was not very great. As early as 1535 Gardiner had written his *De Vera Obedientia,* which is by far the ablest defense of the Royal Supremacy to be published—a book he afterwards came to regret having written—but he did smart over the fact that it was Cranmer, merely the Archdeacon of Taunton, who had been made Archbishop of Canterbury in 1533, an office which Gardiner had every right to feel should have been given to him.

Despite the book that has been mentioned—whose thesis was that the first of Christian duties was to obey the King, and that the King, not the subject, would be answerable to God for royal orders that were excessive—Gardiner was counted as a Bishop of the "Old Learning," and was even thought of as one who might lead a Catholic reaction, should the opportunity for this arise. He became Queen Mary's Chancellor in 1553, but, unfortunately for her, she never quite trusted him, probably on account of the part he had played in trying to obtain the Papal divorce which was Henry VIII's original goal. What is more to the point at the moment is that Gardiner was suspicious of Cranmer's theological tendencies, and quite rightly, even though Cranmer cannot as yet be fairly said to have taken up the definitely heretical attitude of his later years, or the views that were to send him to the stake in 1556.

Perhaps Gardiner was not altogether fair to Cranmer. There were among the newer bishops men far more "advanced" than Cranmer was at this time. Yet it would be equally unfair to Gardiner to ascribe his suspicions to personal motives. There are reasons for believing that even during Henry's lifetime Cranmer worked upon two schemes of a new Church service which, while quite inopportune then, formed the basis of the first Book of Common Prayer introduced when little Edward VI became King. The keen nose of Gardiner smelled something he did not like at all.

The return of Gardiner from one of his many embassies abroad had much to do with the passage by Parliament of the Act of Six Articles. In the House of Lords there were already several bishops of the "New Learning," but one of the peers who was a layman said, "We of the temporality have all been of one mind." Allowing for the possibility of some exaggeration here, it was true enough that even those who had profited by the expropriation of the monasteries (and who had not to some extent?) while usually anti-Papal were also, almost to a man, orthodox in doctrine, lax though many may have been in practice. It is true that Cranmer was to declare in 1549 that the Act would not have passed at all had not the King come personally into the House of Lords to insist upon its passage. Yet even Pollard admits that "This assertion illustrates the sanguine way in which Cranmer under-estimated the forces opposed to him." The vote given in its favor is not re-corded with any rejoicing, for it was much too extreme. It served to frighten heretics, no doubt—which was probably why Gardiner was strongly for it—but one can hardly call it just.

It did undoubtedly indicate that there was a Catholic reaction, though not quite of the right sort. And the Catholic (or perhaps it would be more accurate to say the "conserva-tive") elements in the country achieved, as they imagined, a still greater triumph when the King, having divorced Anne of Cleves, married Katherine Howard in August, 1540. She was a niece of the Duke of Norfolk, and this made her a cousin to Anne Boleyn. She was looked upon as a Catholic, as no doubt she was, in sympathy, scandalous as her past turned out to be. One may also describe her as a protegée of Gardiner, for it was at his house that the King first met her. The Bishop saw to it that Henry and Katherine were thrown a good deal together.

It is a bit comical (and surprising too) that Henry—who at Katharine of Aragon's trial before the Pope's Legates, while never venturing himself to say that she was not a virgin when he married her, or to contradict her vehement assertions that she was, allowed witnesses to appear who strongly implied the contrary—after having been married to four women, should have been totally unaware that Katherine

Howard was anything but virginal. The young woman must not be blamed too severely for her misconduct, for she had been brought up in a rather haphazard fashion by her grandmother, who was not able to exercise much control. The grandmother did catch wind of the fact that young men made their way into the girl's bedroom at night and, learning this, had given her several good beatings. She was, however, most careful to say nothing about this to the King, for to this down-at-the-heel branch of the Howards a royal marriage was the chance of a lifetime. As Queen, Katherine would surely behave herself, and the grandmother counted upon youthful peccadillos never coming to light. At any rate the much experienced married man suspected nothing.

In perfectly good faith Henry accepted her. More than that, he was as much in love with her as such a man could be, even if his "love" was largely the pride of an aging man in a young bride. Katherine was no great beauty, but she was small and dainty—after the big-boned Anne of Cleves, the King had completely got over his idea that a big man, such as he, needed a wife near his own size.* And the stolid Anne, who was so unaccomplished, also was in that respect very unlike this sprightly girl. The King was at first not merely delighted with this Katherine but infatuated. After she had accompanied him on a "progress" through the North, he gave orders, upon their return to Hampton Court, that

---

* It is a rather revealing fact that each of Henry's wives was quite unlike her predecessor. He seems to have picked them with this in mind, always hoping that somehow or other the physical dissimilarity would mean an immense improvement in other respects. Of course he was disappointed every time, never suspecting that *his* might be the fault. Perhaps he cannot be blamed after having been married to the sharp- and loose-tongued Anne Boleyn, with her domineering ways.

a special Mass be said in thanksgiving for their happiness. He was loud in praise of his young bride's "maidenliness."

While the King and Queen were in the North, however, some startling news came to light, and the man selected to tell Henry about it was Cranmer. Yet if he had not done so, somebody else would have borne the tale. Perhaps the Archbishop was chosen as the person most likely to give out the story gently, for Henry was all too likely to be beside himself with rage, but might take from the soft-spoken Cranmer what he would not take from anybody else.

While that extenuation may be made, it must be added that the "new" men were more than ready for poor Katherine to be destroyed. If she was like the rest of the Howards she was indifferent about religion but was thought of as being upon the Catholic side. And she may have been glib enough with pious expressions to have taken Bishop Gardiner in, though one would have thought him too hard-headed to have been easily imposed upon. But coming upon the scene just after the Six Articles, it was feared by those of the New Learning that Katherine might prove more of a menace than the statute itself.

She was not "framed" as Anne Boleyn had been. There can be no question that in her girlhood she had been promiscuous, though one hopes that, after marriage, she intended to be a faithful wife. If so, she showed, even then, astonishing imprudence, for she allowed a couple of her former lovers to see her now and then. Yet there is this to be said: to have sent them packing too decisively might have brought the old scandals to light. Presumably she admitted these men into her presence only to explain why for her sake (and their own) they had better go as far away as possible. She knew that even this kind of an interview was risky, as is shown by the fact that she used Lady Rochford to give warning of the King's approach. This, however, does not necessarily mean that Lady Rochford knew anything about the young Queen's past. When her past did come to light, it is not surprising that it was believed that Katherine was continuing to misbehave herself, with Lady Rochford as an accomplice.

Cranmer was sent to see the Queen at Syon House, where she was at first imprisoned. And in the letter he wrote the King in November, 1541, it is clear that he sincerely pitied her.* He reported that Katherine was well nigh beside herself with terror, as well she might be. But though she did eventually admit to the Archbishop her premarital misconduct, she made out that one of the young men she had allowed to get into her bed had virtually raped her, which seems most unlikely in view of what had been learned from other sources. We are told that she had lain between the sheets with Francis Dereham, the lover in question, " a hundred nights" and that another named Manox "knew a private mark on her body," so we cannot but conclude that the poor young girl in her terror was doing some desperate lying. Cranmer was as kind as possible under the circumstances, saying that Katherine would admit no more than that Dereham had raped her, "without her free will and consent," and as for the precontract whose existence he had tried to establish, he wrote: "I have herewith enclosed all that I can get of her concerning any communication of matrimony with Dereham; which, although it be not so much as I thought, surely, it is sufficient to prove a con-

* *Miscellaneous Writings and Letters of Thomas Cranmer,* Parker Society, 1846, 408–409.

tract, with carnal copulation following; although she think it be no contract as indeed the words alone be not, if carnal copulation had not followed thereof."

Cranmer, on thinking the matter over, must have reached the conclusion that no precontract could be proved, otherwise there would have been ample grounds for a declaration that Katherine's marriage to Henry was null and void, and no such declaration was ever made. We have good reason to doubt the precontract ourselves, but also good reason to doubt that the girlish promiscuity occurred because Katherine was "forced." We may also doubt whether Katherine was guilty of adultery, however often she had in early life committed fornication. Cranmer's letter indicates, without saying so explicity, that he carried Katherine a promise from Henry that her life would be spared, and that it was on the strength of this that she calmed down from her frenzied condition enough to make what admissions she did. That promise, however, was not kept: with Lady Rochford she was executed on February 12, 1542, two of her lovers having already suffered death. The whole performance seems unnecessarily cruel, as the admitted offenses had all been committed prior to marriage, and as Lady Rochford went to the block insane. Adultery may perhaps be presumed, but only because Katherine had been highly injudicious in allowing her former lovers to show themselves at court, however briefly. It seems that Cranmer tried to help the unfortunate girl, though he knew that she was the protegée of Gardiner and Norfolk, the men most strongly opposed to the New Learning.

The Katherine Howard episode did not cause any swing in the direction of the more advanced men, not even doing any discernible harm to Bishop Gardiner who had done what he could to further what had turned out to be a disastrous marriage. The King had, indeed, first met the girl at Gardiner's house, but there were no diplomatic involvements and everything had really been due to Henry's being attracted by a fairly comely girl who belonged to the first family in the land. While her father and grandmother were sent for a while to the Tower, they were soon released, for no charge more serious could be lodged against them than that they had not watched a little minx carefully enough. Gardiner himself could in no way be blamed, for he could not be expected to know anything about the way that young Katherine had carried on.

Though the King was set in his orthodoxy, the exhibition he had made of it in 1539 was too ferocious (and in some ways too absurd) for the Act of Six Articles, the Whip of Six Strings, to be steadily applied. Cranmer, whose natural disposition was moderate—and who, moreover, belonged to the "left wing" of the hierarchy—had, when the Bill was first introduced into Parliament, made some cautious objections when his opinion was asked, but was overruled by the King. Even these objections, since they had been sent to the King in writing, nearly got him into serious trouble, as Ralph Morice, Cranmer's secretary relates the story. Morice said that he was carrying the Archbishop's comments to the King, when the boat in which he was traveling on the Thames was overturned by a bear swimming in the river. The bear-ward is described as being in the employ of the Lady Elizabeth, who, being only five at the most, was surely too young to keep a pet bear. Since the bear-ward is described as a zealous "Papist," it is much more likely that he belonged to the household of the Lady Mary. He rescued the document and, having read it, decided to present it to the Council, in the hope that it would damage Cranmer.* One of the friends of the Archbishop was sufficiently alarmed to offer him a handsome reward if he would surrender it, but the bear-ward would not do so, and was still obdurate when the reward offered was doubled and then tripled. All was in vain, for Cromwell, who had been warned, encountered the man at the door of the Council Chamber and glared so fiercely that the bear-ward trembled and gave up the incriminating document for nothing. In all this there was probably some truth, but the Archbishop had been asked to express his views in writing, and Henry would probably merely have laughed at so much fuss being made over nothing.

That the King would have supported Cranmer is clear from two other incidents, both of them more serious. The Prebendaries of Canterbury lodged complaints that the Archbishop was encouraging the preaching of heresy. Therefore it was proposed to send down to the archdiocese a commission, headed by the conservative Gardiner, to enquire into the state of affairs. But the King happened to be passing Lambeth Palace in his barge and saw Cranmer walking in the gardens. Calling Cranmer to him, he said, in his most genial manner, "Now I know who is the greatest heretic in Kent!" There really was reason for complaint about the special preachers whom Cranmer had appointed, and also because his Commissary, Dr. Nevinson, † was suspected of

* That, at least, is what John Foxe tells us. He may have obtained the story from Morice, but probably colored it a good deal.

† Cranmer was not much addicted to nepotism, but it might be remarked that Nevinson was his brother-in-law. The lady he had married was, by the way, accused of having another husband who was still alive. It seems that it was not too difficult in those days, when communications were rather difficult, to practice bigamy with impunity.

favoring those who denied Transubstantiation, and had released Jane Bocher, who was burned under Edward VI for repudiating the Incarnation. Yet when Cranmer reminded the King that a commission had been appointed to enquire into his alleged misdeeds, Henry in high good humor then and there appointed the Archbishop head of this commission. The least that Cranmer could do was to murmur a protest that it would hardly be seemly for him to be judge of a cause in which he was the principal. Yet the King swept the objection aside with, "It shall be no otherwise, for surely I reckon that you will tell me the truth; yea, of yourself, if you have offended." While granting that Cranmer was a man of honesty, no man, surely, is fit to sit in judgment on himself. It may be imagined what kind of decision the commission reached.

Cromwell was evidently right in telling Cranmer that, whatever he did, the King would see to it that condonation was given, whereas Cromwell—and this he did not tell the Archbishop—received a good cudgeling from the royal hands. Cromwell's actual words are worth quoting to make this plain: "You were born in a happy hour; for do and say what you will, the King will always take it well at your hand. And I must needs confess that in some things I have complained of you unto his Majesty, but all in vain, for he will never give credit against you, whatever is laid to your charge; but let me or any other of the Council be complained of, his Grace will most seriously chide and fall out with us. And therefore you are happy if you can keep you in this estate."

An incident that Shakespeare makes use of in his *Henry VIII* (though placing it about 1535, whereas it really occurred nearer to 1545) * has the same indication of favor

---

* We know that it could not have been later because Dr. Butts, the King's physician, died in 1545, and he figures in the incident.

being extended to Cranmer under any circumstances. A complaint had been lodged against the Archbishop in the Council, and Cranmer had been summoned for a hearing, the intention, however, being to send him to the Tower—on what grounds we are not informed, though we can infer it was because his heretical tendencies were gradually becoming more pronounced. Knowing what the Council's plan was, the King gave Cranmer a ring, the production of which would ensure his immunity. Again Morice, as touched up by Foxe, is our authority, so perhaps all this should be taken with a grain of salt.

The next day, when Cranmer presented himself, the members of the Council were unmannerly enough to keep the Archbishop at the door of the room in which they made their deliberations, though this meant that Cranmer had to stand waiting among a crowd of lackeys. Somebody told Dr. Butts about it, and the Doctor first went to keep him company, holding him in conversation, so that the treatment he was accorded should not be remarked. But when the delay became too long, Dr. Butts went to tell the King what was happening.

Henry was (or pretended to be) very indignant, and said afterwards that he had yielded only because the Council had represented to him that nobody would dare to testify against so highly placed a personage as the Archbishop while he was still at large. He stalked down to the Council himself, to find that Cranmer had by that time been brought before it and had been told that he was infecting the whole realm with heretical ideas. But Cranmer had already produced the ring, much to their consternation, Lord Russell exclaiming, "Did I not tell you, my Lords, what would come of this matter? The King would never permit my Lord

of Canterbury to have such a blemish as to be imprisoned."
The Councillors, upon Henry's arrival, tried to make excuses, the Duke of Norfolk—probably the originator of the
scheme—offering the lame excuse that they had meant to
send the Archbishop to the Tower only for a few days, "so
that he might have the greater glory of a triumphant acquittal." Henry affected to accept the excuse, but told them
roundly, "Well, I pray you use not my friends so. I per-
ceive well enough how the world goeth among you. There
remaineth malice among you one to another; let it be avoided
out of hand, I would advise you."

Morice went on to say that after that nobody dared to
bring any charges against the Archbishop during King
Henry's lifetime. That much is certainly true: Henry VIII
meant to be Cranmer's protector, though even Henry would
have made short work of him had he known what position
he was eventually to take up. But while Cranmer probably
was drawing nearer this position, he had not reached it yet.
Obsequious though the man was, it would not be fair to
accuse him, on the strength of the evidence we have, of
downright hypocrisy. Perhaps he had already gone further,
in his private thoughts, than the orthodox King suspected,
but we can only infer this; in his public capacity, he was
still a Catholic—of the Henrician sort. There were some
bishops who, because they went further than Cranmer did
at this time, were forced to resign—Latimer and Shaxton
for example. But Henry was so fond of Cranmer as to put
up with almost anything; and Cranmer, for his part, was
fond of Henry as a man, as well as very obedient to him
as King. He is not to be explained simply as a sycophant.
He honestly believed that the King had now taken the

place of the Pope, and was endowed with spiritual as well as temporal authority.

One reason, and perhaps among the most important of reasons, that Cranmer always remained on such good terms with the King is that he took a very slight part in secular politics, a part so slight it is hardly worth mentioning at all. The complaints that Cromwell confessed he had sometimes brought against Cranmer (to have them brushed aside) could not have been on the grounds of heresy, for it was Cromwell rather than Cranmer who was surreptitiously working in a Protestant direction. At most Cranmer acted merely as an accessory, particularly in the abortive attempt to reach common ground with the Lutheran princes of Germany. As that was political in motive, the King knew and approved of what was being done, up to a point. One cannot but suspect that Cromwell's allusions were to the presence in Lambeth of Mrs. Cranmer, concerning whom Henry had probably been informed already, but had decided to do nothing, so long as Cranmer kept his German wife out of sight. Then she could be conveniently considered as no more than an "uncanonical wife," such as other priests had—which was reprehensible but winked at. Though Cromwell could have made trouble about her after Parliament passed the Act of Six Articles, perhaps not even Cromwell could have made very serious trouble. At all events Henry himself came forward as the Archbishop's protector, even when people like the Prebendaries of Canterbury were making complaints about Cranmer's heretical tendencies, as these tendencies could not be very definite. After Cromwell's fall, Cranmer was able to take his difficulties direct to the King, whom he did not find it very difficult to deal with, especially since Mrs. Cranmer had been sent back in a hurry to Nuremberg. Despite what might have been expected, Cranmer's position was eased by the loss of a dictatorial protector. It became clear that the King, being on most cordial terms with the Archbishop was not going to allow anybody to trouble him again.

Chapter Twelve

The End of the Old King

Henry VIII was not really old when he died, only fifty-six, an age which we reckon as the prime of life, or late middle age. But he had abused his body by his Gargantuan eating and drinking, though not by sexual over-indulgence. At least we may consider him—as he considered himself—rather virtuous in this respect, for though he had had six wives, we know of only two mistresses, both of them before Anne Boleyn appeared upon the scene, Elizabeth Blount and Mary Boleyn, which is a rather good record for kings in those days, and is even a rather good record for some kings of today. Froude suggests that Henry was, upon the whole, somewhat lacking in virility, and he is probably right; the true explanation of his many marital adventures should be looked for in his anxiety to have a male heir, though no doubt he wished to have other sons beside Edward, as he was aware that the Tudor princes did not have much expectation of long life. Henry's brother Arthur died when he was only about fifteen, and his own sole bastard, the Duke of Richmond, died at seventeen. Though Henry's vanity should not be left out of account, we remain with the impression that this ordinarily manifested itself in a relatively innocent philandering by which he could prove that he was not unattractive to women, but which did not go further than that. This seems borne out by the fact that Anne Boleyn caught him one day with a lady-in-waiting sitting on his knee and furiously berated him for it. His reply, that she had better learn to put up with what her betters (meaning Katharine of Aragon) had done, indicates that he had been what we may call flirtatious during Katharine's time and that she had not made any great fuss about it. For that matter his two mistresses were taken while Katharine was the recognized Queen, and (with her father in mind) she had accepted this as the ordinary behavior of kings, for she continued to bear him children in rapid succession long afterwards, though of these all except Mary died. Evidently the extremely pious and virtuous Katharine regarded mistresses as a matter of course, as what might be expected of a man, though she did not like it. But after Anne Boleyn, we hear of no mistresses, only of some amorous playfulness.

This needs to be said because the usual view is that Henry VIII was a lecherous monster. Certainly it was true that in his later years he was prematurely old, looking and acting about fifteen years older than he actually was. When he married the widow Katherine Parr—after Katherine Howard he was going to take no chances with another "virgin"—it was mainly because he needed a wife who would be a nurse, as England at that time had no nurses in our sense of the word, or any of any competence. This last wife also was a well-educated and clever woman, able to keep the King amused and also to hide from him the fact that she had a strong tendency towards the New Learning.

Discussions about Catholic practices and spoliations went on to the end of the reign, though Henry would not permit any tampering with the Mass, for which he felt great veneration. After the death of Jane Seymour, which occurred when Cromwell was busy with his program of loot, Henry founded a convent to pray for the repose of her soul, and his will provided that Masses be said for him in perpetuity. This runs contradictory to Morice's report that Cranmer had told him the King was meditating reducing the divine service to something similar to what was in the first Book of Common Prayer. It is quite possible that Cranmer did say something like this, but it only shows again that he was all too disposed to be sanguine. However, the immensely rich shrine of St. Thomas à Becket at Canterbury was denuded of its treasures on the ground that St. Thomas, by setting himself in opposition to Henry II, had shown himself a traitor. Even when no treason was involved—as in the case of the shrines of Our Lady of Walsingham, St. Dunstan at Winchester, and St. Cuthbert at Durham—a reason was found for loot: they promoted superstition!

It may be true that what had brought matters to this pass was not rejection of Catholic doctrine but disgust with the exactions of some of the clergy. While these exactions were often real enough, a point chosen for attack (or at least questioning) on the part of the more advanced men, was that of "private Masses," about which a word of explanation should be given. There is nothing that obliges a priest to say Mass every day, unless it be for his parishioners, and though almost every priest does in fact say a daily Mass, this is by way of devotion. These are often said with only an altar-boy in attendance, and for many of these Masses an offering is made—which definitely is not payment—that the infinite merits of the Mass be for a departed soul. Should such an offering be made, there is the most binding of obligations on the priest who accepts it, except that he is free to pass on the offering (and the obligation) to another priest.

It is, however, easy to see how some came to believe that the saying of Masses for private intentions gave priests too great a hold over people. While the Mass itself was in no way attacked at first, the power of the clergy who said the Mass was resented, and from that point it spread to become, eventually, an attack on the Mass itself. Though this would have been regarded with horror by Henry, he was nevertheless responsible for creating an atmosphere inimical to all that he, to the end of his life, looked upon as sacred.

Cranmer was, as usual, careful what he said about controversial points, and not merely points upon which he and the King would have got to loggerheads. He was not of the truculently argumentative type but wished to live at peace with everybody. When he left Cambridge University, and even when he became Archbishop of Canterbury, he did not remotely resemble a Protestant. He was merely one who thought—as, perhaps, the majority of English people thought—that the Pope's authority should be curtailed and the King's enlarged. But there are indications that his religious opinions were, by now, veering away from orthodoxy, even if they were not as yet heterodox. The complaints brought against him at least suggest this. And when, after the battle of Solway Moss at the end of 1542, one of the chief Scottish prisoners, the young Earl of Cassilis, was given a very pleasant sort of incarceration at Lambeth Palace, the conversations this man had with his host (or jailor) may have had some bearing upon the Reformation in Scotland.

Yet we may attribute too much here to Cranmer, in view of the earlier history of the Earl of Cassilis. Shortly before, in Paris, the Earl had had as his tutor George Buchanan, who became the best of Scottish Latin poets, and who left the Collège de Sainte-Barbare to accept this job.

Even at that time Buchanan was suspected of heretical leanings and by the mid-century he openly joined the Reformers.
He is rather more than suspected of having had a main part
in the forgery of the Casket Letters used to besmirch Mary
Queen of Scots. An unsavory man but of acute intelligence,
he could not have failed to have left his mark upon the
Earl. But as Cassilis died in his thirties he probably did
not do much for the Reformation in Scotland; and the fact
that he was sent as one of the commissioners to France when
the youthful Queen of Scots married the Dauphin suggests
that he was at that time nominally orthodox, though a
heretical tendency may have existed since he was under
the charge of Buchanan. It is not likely that Cranmer would
have actively encouraged this, not at this time, and surely
not under these circumstances.

During the last years of Henry VIII's life, Cranmer took
a more active part in politics, but this was still on a relatively small scale and did not mean much more than that
he appeared fairly frequently at the Council, no doubt at
the King's request. For example, it was Cranmer who was
asked to tell the French Ambassador that it would be con-
ducive to peace if France did not proceed further with
its fortifications near Calais, which had been started before
1540. The obvious answer was that the English should
strengthen their own fortifications, which showed signs of
needing repair. But Henry disliked spending the money
filched from the monasteries on such projects, though he
was to fight two useless wars before he died—a war being
showy and a good excuse for asking Parliament for a special
subsidy. If Henry had only strengthened Calais, it would
almost certainly have been safely retained during the hapless
Mary's reign.

When in 1544 King Henry crossed the Channel to take personal command of his army in a futile war, a new suit of armor had to be made for the bulky old man, and in this he pranced about almost as though he were young again, but, as when young, he took good care not to expose himself to any danger. Then Cranmer was appointed to the Council of Regency to advise the new Queen. This was of course Katherine Parr, who, not much over thirty and already twice a widow, was to marry again for the fourth time only a month or so after the King's death. To this fourth husband, Thomas Seymour, who was Henry's brother-in-law she bore her first child, dying in child-bed. She was a rather learned woman and got on excellently with the Lady Mary, to whom she was perhaps even kinder than Jane Seymour had been. As we hear nothing about Mary's relations with Katherine Howard, one is led to suspect that Mary at once saw through her, though it must be remembered that Mary saw little of her, and nothing at all during that royal "progress" through the North when the damning evidence was being assiduously assembled. She was by that time a little older than her new stepmother. Katherine Howard was supposed to be the Catholic hope, whereas Katherine Parr was suspected of heretical leanings. Yet it was with the last of Henry's Katherines that the Lady Mary struck up her friendship, which may, perhaps, be taken as showing some good qualities in this lady. Qualities that were not so admirable appeared after the old King's death. While he lived she was assiduous in her attendance upon him, in the correspondence by which she and Mary practiced their Latin, and also in translating into English part of the *Paraphrases* of Erasmus and persuading Mary to do the same. For her susceptibility to men she is not to be fairly blamed—but perhaps to be commended; at least nothing against her morals could be adduced. It may well be that the King took her as his sixth and last wife because she could not make the faintest pretense of virginity; the absurd, prematurely old man picked her out as one likely to be ardent in the marital bed.

Be this as it may, fire still smouldered in the man: at times he could be quite magnificent. One of these times was when he addressed Parliament not much more than a year before his death, and what was remarkable in his speech was not merely its force but its good sense and tolerant spirit. We may almost take it as a swan-song when he said (the quotation is given only in part): "I hear that the special foundation of our religion, being charity between man and man, is so refrigerate as there was never more lack of love between man and man, the occasion whereof are opinions only and names for the continuing of the same. Some are called Papists, some Lutherans, and some Anabaptists; names devised of the devil, and yet not fully without ground, for the severing of one man's heart by conceit of opinion from the other. For the remedy whereof, I desire, first every man of himself to travail first for his own amendment. Secondly, I exhort the bishops and clergy, who are noted to be the salt and the lamps of the world, by amending their divisions, to give example to the rest, and to agree especially in their teaching—which, seeing there is but one truth and verity, they may easily do, calling therein for the aid of God. Finally, I exhort the nobles and the lay fee not to receive the Grace of God in vain; and albeit, by the instinct of God, the Scriptures have been permitted them in the English tongue, yet to take upon themselves the judgment and exposition of the same, but reverendly and humbly, with fear and dread, to receive the use and knowledge which it hath pleased God to show unto them, and in any doubt to resort unto the learned, or at best the higher powers. I am very sorry to hear how that precious jewel the Word of God is disputed, rhymed, sung and jangled in every alehouse and tavern. . . . Of this I am sure, that charity was never so faint among you; and God Himself, among Christians, was never less reverenced, honored and served. Therefore, as I said before, be in charity with one another, like brother and brother. . . . Then may I justly rejoice that thus long I have lived to see this day, and you, by verity, conscience and charity between yourselves, may in this point, as you be in others, accounted among the rest of the world as blessed men."

The words are splendid, but it is obvious that it never crossed the mind of the man, who must have known that he would soon die, that he, more than anybody else, was responsible for the devastation he now deplored. Could one expect of a tyrannical old egotist anything else? But at least it is a good deal that he had noted the devastation, and at the last moment tried to amend it—without, of course, using the only means of correction. But clearly he was apprehensive of what would happen when he was gone, though he tried to control this by drawing a careful and detailed will, in the illusion that his successors would not be able to interpret it in the way that best suited themselves.

Even before he died, Anne Askew, who earlier had been charged with denying Transubstantiation but who had been protected by Cranmer's Commissary, was arrested again on the old charge, of which she was plainly guilty under the existing law, and with her was arrested ex-Bishop Shaxton. While commiserating with them, we should not forget that it was largely at Henry's insistence that the Act of Six Articles was passed by Parliament in 1539. Bishop Bonner (Foxe's "Bloody Bonner") persuaded Shaxton, whose heresy could not have been very extreme since he was a suffragan bishop under Queen Mary, to recant. Anne Askew remained fanatical in her defiance though she was so terribly racked she had to be carried to the stake in a chair. The preacher, on that occasion, was none other than Shaxton, whom Anne kept interrupting with sarcastic comments; but into the fire she went.

It may be supposed that the kindly Cranmer was not very happy about her, but his own affairs had grown easier. He may have sighed now and then as he thought of his quiet days in Cambridge University, and he is recorded as saying that, though as Archbishop he was reckoned a rich man, there were so many drains and demands made upon him that he had been better off as a university Don. However, we may treat this as the kind of grumbling every man makes occasionally, not intending it to be taken very seriously. He had come safely through his dangers. But it would indeed have been better for him to have been left as a Fellow of Jesus College, obscure, secure and content.

The King was a loyal friend, but was growing old. Cranmer did not know how he would fare under the new men he noticed to be emerging. Katherine Parr's brother, a rapscallion who had been given Cromwell's old title of the Earl of Essex, did not count for much, though he survived to be one of the Councilors of Queen Elizabeth, by whom he was created Marquis of Northampton. The men who did count were John Dudley—at this time Viscount Lisle, who was to rise to be Earl of Warwick and then Duke of Northumberland—and the uncles of Prince Edward, the elder of

whom was to become Duke of Somerset and the Protector—
and William Paget, the King's secretary and chief adviser.
These were able men, but very ambitious ones, and it was
a question as to how far they could be trusted. But Cranmer made a kind of tacit alliance with Edward Seymour,
the best of the bunch, the one with whom he had most in
common. This dreamy soul was to show that he could not
maintain his ground against the ruthless Dudley, but Cranmer was too sanguine to be realistic, and probably did not
dream of the upheavals that were ahead. It is at least to
his credit that he was distrustful of Dudley.

Yet the Seymours themselves could be ruthless. As the
Duke of Norfolk was the greatest personage in the country,
he had to be ruined. This was not hard to effect because of
his son, the Earl of Surrey, the famous poet. One would
have thought that even the most indiscreet man would have
known better than to quarter any of the royal emblems on
his coat-of-arms. This was taken as tantamount to treason
so Surrey was beheaded. Even his old father, who had
given so many services to the Crown over a long period of
years was condemned and escaped the block only because
the King died the day before the Duke's execution was
scheduled. Even so, Norfolk was kept in the Tower until
the accession of Mary; a man like that, with a large following
among the older nobility could not safely be left at large.
Besides, he was looked upon as the leader of the Catholic
party, slight as was his interest in religion. Cranmer, though
he had no share in the Howards' ruin, at least knew that
his best understanding could be reached with Edward
Seymour.

A period of tumult might arise when the old King died,
but Cranmer clung to the consoling thought that the new

King, though he was only a child, would be nominally head of the Church. Ecclesiastical government would therefore continue to lie in the hands of lay rulers—which was where it ought to be. He may have feared that those who ruled in the little King's name would be rapacious. Henry himself was of course highly rapacious, but had moments of generosity and, what was more important, was a man of genuine religious feeling. Edward Seymour seemed to be, or posed as being, very religious. That was why Cranmer threw his lot in with him.

Ralph Morice later reported that Cranmer had told him that Henry meditated further changes in religion. This is very doubtful, but it is possible that, as the old King foresaw that some changes would occur, he thought it safest to introduce them himself—when they would be slight—than leave the matter to men who would probably be more drastic. But this may be merely another instance of Cranmer's being too sanguine about the orthodox Henry. It suggests, however, that at the end of the reign the Archbishop was more than ready to support such changes, and it is quite likely that he gave Edward Seymour some hint of this.

Actually the greatest change that eventuated was Cranmer's production of the Litany of 1545. Subsequently the invocation of the Blessed Virgin was dropped as being too Catholic, and the invocations of Patriarchs * were omitted, perhaps because they did not have much appeal, even to Protestants. The offensive prayer—"From the tyranny of the Bishop of Rome and all his detestable enormities"—disap-

* The introduction of Old Testament characters, instead of Catholic saints, in Cranmer's projected revision of the Breviary strongly suggests that he had worked upon it even while Henry was alive, though perhaps in secret. More will be said about this later.

149

peared under Elizabeth. But Cranmer's Litany, as we know it, well deserves all the admiration it has received. One must admit that it is a great work of literature, and from that point of view is an improvement upon the Latin litanies with their monotonous repetition of *Ora pro nobis*. Yet this litany is hardly to be considered a doctrinal revolution. The religious situation in England had not become very different from what it was after the breach with the Holy See in 1534, except that denunciations of the Pope had been dinned into the people's ears.

Even had Cranmer not reached in advance some working agreement with Edward Seymour, he undoubtedly surmised that there would be changes, though Henry VIII laid it down most explicitly in his will that no alteration in religion was to be introduced before his son Edward was twenty-four. For it is only in human nature to wish for some change, if everything depends upon a secular ruler. Henry VIII had been King for such a long while and had shown himself so masterful—not to say tyrannical—that a new regime would be sure to wish to order things in a new fashion. Edward Seymour, who had the shrewd Paget to advise him, as the elder of Prince Edward's two uncles would be his natural guardian. We know him to have been an unstable man, mouthing the cant phrases of something very like Calvinism (at least it resembled Puritanism), and he had a Welsh necromancer attached to his household. At least that was true of him later. So long as Henry was alive he made Catholic professions. But it may be taken for granted that Edward Seymour wished to have a free hand, and had already thought out what he would do as soon as the old King died. How far he and Cranmer confided in one another must be largely conjectural, but in all probability Seymour "sounded" Cranmer, just as Cranmer had quite correctly reached the conclusion that Edward Seymour was bound to obtain control and was much to be preferred to Dudley, his most formidable rival.

One more thing should be said about the Seymour brothers: while the elder, Edward, was strait-laced (which did not prevent him from being rapacious) his younger brother Thomas was a loose-liver, a notorious lady-killer. Edward had charge of the education of the boy who was to be King, carefully educating him in general knowledge (in which he was precocious) but in particular to ascend the throne when his father died. He made the boy into a prig and fanatic, which was not fortunate; but Thomas Seymour would have been a most deplorable guide in the opposite direction. These facts had much to do with subsequent happenings.

Henry VIII's will, which was dated December 30, 1546, less than a month before his death, invoked Our Lady and all the Saints, and provided that he be buried beside Jane Seymour in the chapel at Windsor Castle. It also made it clear that, whatever Cranmer may have told Morice, Henry died a Catholic—that is, a Catholic in his own style—and that he wished England to remain Catholic, in the Henrician sense. Also he named Mary and Elizabeth—though he had bastardized them both by statute—as those who were to succeed their half-brother, in the event of his dying childless. The claims of any descendants of his sister Margaret, who had married a king of Scotland, were absolutely ruled out.

The old King happened to die on January 27, 1547, when the members of Parliament had gone home, which perfectly suited the convenience of the Council, who were thus left unhampered. While Cranmer, hurriedly summoned from

151

Croydon, was kneeling by the King, who was by that time hardly conscious, Edward Seymour and Paget were pacing the long gallery, planning their first move. The Archbishop no doubt asked a few questions of the dying man—such as any confessor would ask—but he could get no word in reply, only an answer by a pressure upon his hands. One account—which need not be believed, as nobody was present —is that Henry at last muttered, "All is lost." Another account says that the King's last words were something about Our Lady of Walsingham. Cranmer could have repeated either thing, as it did not involve breaking the seal of confession. Most likely Cranmer himself was not quite sure what the thick, throttled voice really said.

Chapter Thirteen

The New Regime

The death of Henry VIII was kept secret for several days. To make sure that the news would be hidden, only two or three people were allowed into the room where the corpse lay; among these was the King's doctor, because if he stayed away somebody might guess the truth. He therefore came and went several times a day, as though in attendance upon a sick man, but he was pledged to the strictest secrecy, and he knew that he was now dealing with men who would know how to deal with him if he allowed the slightest word to escape.

What was occurring was really a "palace revolution," and Edward Seymour and Paget had planned how to carry it out, while they were pacing the long gallery waiting for the old King to die. Seymour was to place himself under the direction of the more experienced Paget, but it was Seymour who was to hold the actual reins of government, and who made a promise that he would curb his propensity to mildness.

Paget gave out—what may have been true but is open to some doubt—that Henry VIII had intended to confer some new titles, and these on Paget's unsupported word were distributed. It may have been only to give plausibility to what he said, that Sir Thomas Wriothesley, the Lord Chancellor but soon afterwards ejected from office, was raised to the peerage. Edward Seymour, already Earl of Hereford, became the Duke of Somerset and the Lord Protector. His younger brother would, it was hoped, be placated by being made a baron and the Lord High Admiral. Paget, a man of thirty-five, of relatively low birth, was advanced a rung; as he had been Henry VIII's close associate during the past four years, he was invaluable to the new regime.

Seymour's Protectorate was of course in flat contravention of Henry's will, for those he had named as his executors were to be on an equal footing, and also were to constitute the Council, whereas under Seymour's plan, the Protector was empowered to act with or without the consent of the Council, just as though he were actually the King. To carry the plot through, Seymour rode at once to where Edward VI was staying, woke the boy up in the early hours of the morning, and ordered him to accompany him to London. It was essential that he get the new King into his hands at once. We may be sure that Cranmer was not given any inkling of all this, for though any scruples he expressed would have been disregarded, it was not regarded as any of his business.

Cranmer may also have disapproved of the Protectorate, though as he had formed a kind of tacit alliance with Edward Seymour, he was hardly able to make any very strong objections. Nor could any member of the Council voice much disapproval—not after Seymour had obtained possession of the little boy who was to be the new King. After all, the man was Edward's natural guardian. John Dudley was probably furious at the march stolen upon him, but for the moment he too had ostensibly to accept the situation.

If Dudley had vast ambitions, so also had the younger

154

Seymour, now Baron Seymour of Sudeley, though his technique was quite different. He must have smiled to himself, thinking of how his ends were to be achieved. He lost no time in proposing marriage to Lady Mary, but he must have expected her refusal, for when it was given, he wrote asking her aid in obtaining Henry's widow as his wife. Mary refused again, on the ground that she knew nothing about love or courtship, and as Katherine Parr had been a former "flame" of the Admiral's, she might be counted upon to marry him now.

The judgment was perfectly sound. The Admiral was not yet forty, a handsome and vigorous man, who would be a welcome change after a prematurely old semi-invalid. But the lovers knew they could not expect the immediate consent of the Council, as it was possible that Katherine was with child by Henry VIII. If she immediately conceived a child by the Admiral, the question might be raised whether her child was not really the dead King's and therefore in the line of succession. But clandestine meetings occurred, Katherine admitting the Admiral by a postern-gate in her garden at Chelsea, and he creeping away at break of dawn. There was some danger that these comings and goings might be observed, and a still greater risk that she might conceive. However, the pious and learned lady, being also amorous, took it, and, as it happened, without detection. After enjoying such dalliance for a month or two, they applied for the Council's permission to do what they had already done; and by that time permission was forthcoming.

In Thomas Seymour's case he was not actuated solely by a wish to marry Katherine Parr. The Queen-Mother had staying at her house at Chelsea her step-daughter (if she can be called such), the Lady Elizabeth, a girl who, as she was now fourteen, was considered almost nubile. The Admiral, let us hope, had no plan of getting rid of Katherine in some way, and then of marrying Elizabeth, but was only exercising his propensity for making love to any woman he encountered. But the possibility of the darkest of designs cannot be dismissed in the case of a man of his sort; he would not have balked at a murder, if it could be made to look like an accident.

Let us not make any charges, but look upon the affair as no worse than a gross impropriety. Elizabeth was accompanied by her governess, Katherine Ashley, from whom comes most of our knowledge of what happened. And while Mrs. Ashley, under other circumstances, might have made a vigorous protest, what could she say when the Queen was merely amused at what the Admiral did? We hear that nearly every morning he used to make his way into Elizabeth's bedroom before she was up—sometimes accompanied by the Queen, but sometimes alone—and that then he would playfully tickle Elizabeth, or even slap her buttocks while she lay in bed. If, laughing, she drew further into the bed, they would go after her, Katherine laughing at the good clean fun. Mrs. Ashley says that on one occasion, when Elizabeth was wearing a black dress (woman-like Mrs. Ashley remembered that detail), the Queen held her while the Admiral cut the dress to shreds. Elizabeth made a show of putting up a struggle, but it was only a show, and though the Queen would no doubt have objected had there been more than this, it could be that Seymour did proceed further when Katherine and Mrs. Ashley were not present. One wonders whether it was during these "rompings," as they

were called, that Elizabeth discovered she had a sexual mal-
formation that made full congress impossible.*

Katherine Parr took some part in these goings-on, which
may prove that, while indelicate, they were innocent enough,
or that Katherine herself was perhaps rather indelicate. However, she evidently came to the conclusion that her husband
was not to be trusted with Elizabeth, or that a girl who was
in the line of royal succession should not be exposed to such
dangers while under her roof. So she and the Admiral moved
elsewhere, Katherine dying soon afterwards in childbirth,
her first in four marriages. Following the lady's death, Mrs.
Ashley suggested that Elizabeth write Thomas Seymour a
letter of condolence. But Elizabeth knew that the Admiral
would not be overwhelmed with grief and so refused, with
blunt honesty, so that Mrs. Ashley was obliged to write the
letter herself.

Still more has to be recorded. The Admiral persuaded the
Marquis of Dorset—who was soon to be created a Duke—
to make his daughter, Lady Jane Grey, his ward. It is astonishing that any parents would entrust their daughter to
such a man, but the inducement held out was that Edward
VI's uncle would get the King to marry her as soon as he
(and the girl) reached marriageable age, which in those days
was very early. Thomas Seymour had ingratiated himself
with the King by giving him lavish tips, with a good slice
for Sir John Cheke, his tutor. These tips were slipped un-

---

* I do not believe I am one to take gossip very seriously, but many
of Queen Elizabeth's contemporaries were very explicit, and at least
some of them were in a position to know. I mention merely the names
of Drummond of Hawthornden, Sir Walter Raleigh, Lady Shrewsbury
and Brantôme, though of course, even if what they said of Elizabeth
was true, there is no means of knowing that this was discovered during her "rompings" with Thomas Seymour.

der the carpet at an agreed-upon place and the young King used them for betting, something of which his other (and Puritanical) uncle disapproved. Though Edward was himself being most strictly brought up, and had many pious expressions on his lips, he also used such bad language at times that people wondered where he could have learned the words. We can easily guess where. The boy was a strange mixture, for he was being so thoroughly indoctrinated with the most advanced Protestant ideas as to be a precocious theologian of a most unpleasant sort. John Lingard, the Catholic historian, even thinks that the Church of England, as we know it, escaped much by Edward's early death. Though betting is harmless enough, in itself, and many boys pass safely through a phase of foul language, these were not consistent with what the Protector was aiming at.

Cranmer of course knew little, if anything, about such matters. He saw the boy only rarely, and then of course the young King was on his very best behavior. The Archbishop of Canterbury was fully occupied with other concerns. In any event he had never dabbled much in secular politics. But in one way he had greatly changed: as a mark of perpetual sorrow for Henry VIII, for whom he had sincere affection, he never shaved after the old King's death, so that eventually he attained a long, if somewhat untidy, beard. One would hardly think that this later Cranmer and the Cranmer in the painting of the National Portrait Gallery were the same person.

However Cranmer, as a member of the Council, though he did not regularly attend, heard something about the doings of the Admiral. These did not end with what has been already recorded. For it came out that this man, though supposedly in charge of the royal navy, had entered into an arrangement with the pirates who had their nest in the Scilly Isles. Furthermore, he had persuaded Sharrington, the Comptroller of the Bristol Mint, to give him a special supply of coinage. It became evident that Thomas Seymour was preparing to resort to armed rebellion, if this was necessary for the gaining of his ends. Such conduct was downright treason, and though Somerset might have saved his brother by a quasi-royal pardon, he let him go to the block. Of course the man was guilty of devious crimes (or was it not rather harebrained foolishness?) but there were some of Somerset's enemies who were secretly delighted that the Protector should incur the odium of executing a brother. Some odium, however, should fall upon the young King who did nothing for his uncle, but only recorded his execution in a single cold sentence in his diary, while Elizabeth's comment was, "This day died a man with much wit and little judgment." Thomas Seymour had banked upon all of them. But as Somerset was the Protector, this fact was used before long as one of the means by which his enemies pulled him down.

That Somerset had obtained a good deal of popularity in rural England by opposing the enclosure movement also went against him with the newly rich, as Paget bluntly told him. Yet the "Good Duke," as some of the peasants called him, was so rapacious in London that he demolished a number of churches to use their thick stone walls in the building of his palace. The famous Dance of Death which had been one of the sights in St. Paul's Cathedral was used for this purpose, and only the gathering of a threatening mob saved St. Margaret's, Westminster. The Abbey itself only escaped destruction because a big bribe was offered. The Good Duke was a strange character, and his portrait shows

a long narrow melancholy face with long drooping musta-
chios, which one would think belonged to a poet rather
than a tyrant. But he was something of a tyrant, and a very
irascible one. In short he had a considerable gift for an-
tagonizing people, so that almost from the start his eventual downfall was certain.

That anybody should have called him the "Good Duke"
is hard to understand, unless Somerset seemed good only in
comparison with others. Professor Pollard, writing Somerset's life in 1900, credits him with idealism and with having a social program in advance of the age. If this was really
so, the age must have been exceptionally wicked, or at least
exceptionally greedy. Of course Henry VIII, under Cromwell's guidance, had started the looting, so perhaps it is not
very surprising that the men now in power, with only a
child as King, should have been eager to get their hot,
heavy hands upon what the old King had allowed to remain. During the first year that little Edward was on the
throne the Chantries Act was passed. One cannot assert that
the property of all the guilds was confiscated, nor were all
Masses for the dead abolished—yet. Professedly, the only
funds confiscated were those being used for a "superstitious"
purpose, and these were supposed to be transferred to the
Crown for the founding of schools. But it was not difficult
to regard any purpose as superstitious when it was a question of taking possession of revenues, which, in aggregate,
were vast. As for the "King Edward VI Grammar Schools"
still in existence, which many fondly believe were founded
in Edward's time, they are merely the few that were permitted to survive. This saying is often attributed to R. H.
Tawney, who probably did use it in one of his books, but
he was quoting William Cobbett without giving due attri-

bution. Cranmer was distressed by all this and voted against the Chantries Act, but except for that he was powerless. He was to be still more distressed when Somerset, who probably did have a streak of idealism in him, was crushed by the abler Northumberland, a ruffian whom nobody has ever been able to credit with anything but the seeking of his own advantage.

One must say that under the Somerset regime there was no direct religious persecution, and for this perhaps Cranmer should be given some credit, though he believed (as everybody did) in the principle of religious persecution and before the end of Edward's reign was to prepare a new code which made even the belief in Transubstantiation a heretical offense punishable by death. But by temperament he was mild, and he advocated the repeal of Henry's more ferocious laws on the subject. Early in the reign he made a speech to Convocation in which he urged the clergy to study the Bible and to consider "what things were in the Church that needed reformation." When to this the answer promptly came that as long as the Six Articles were on the statute book, it was dangerous to express an opinion (which was perfectly true), Cranmer worked for the reduction of treason to the moderate definition it had had under Edward III, for the repeal of all heresy acts since Richard II, and for giving royal proclamations the force of law. Also there was to be full liberty to discuss religious questions, to print the Bible in English, and to publish theological works. Of course it cannot be claimed for Cranmer that he deserves more than a part of the credit; also in actual practice there was not nearly so much liberty as the wording of the new statutes might suggest. Joan Bocher was burned at the stake in 1550 for denying the Incarnation, and of course everywhere—not only in England—Anabaptists received no mercy.

Henry VIII was given a grand requiem, which was sung by Cranmer, as Archbishop, in full regalia. And when Francis I died a few months later there was another requiem sung by Cranmer, assisted by a number of other bishops. It was perhaps significant that the sermon preached on that occasion—by Bishop Ridley (of Rochester, at the time)—laid its main stress upon the French translation of the Bible that Francis had permitted. Catholics of course had no objection anywhere to a vernacular rendering of the Bible—not in itself—but everywhere these vernacular renderings were used to promote heresy, though it must be said that the French King, a notoriously loose-living man, seems to have had the idea that he could even his score with God by burning heretics even more freely that Henry did.

At Edward's coronation the long elaborate ceremonies were abbreviated as being too much for a child. Belloc exaggerates somewhat in describing the sermon Cranmer preached then as a declaration of the "divine right of kings." At most it maintained no more than Henry had held, and probably rather less.* In less than a page and a half Cranmer could hardly develope in full the doctrine we associate with James I. Naturally he repudiates the Pope's authority; that was only the law of the land. Nor does there seem to be much harm in saying that he thinks Edward will turn out to be a "second Josiah," though that may be slightly absurd. But he does tell the young King what he would never have ventured to tell his father: "As a messenger from Jesus Christ, I shall most humbly admonish

* A report of this sermon is in the *Miscellaneous Writings and Letters of Thomas Cranmer.*

your royal Majesty, what things your Highness is to perform." But of course Cranmer was an elderly man addressing a small boy.

As a matter of fact, Cranmer did sometimes admonish the young King, but only when the Protector and the Council knew what he was going to say and permitted the Archbishop to speak. The actual control, even of spiritual matters was less in his hands than theirs. The whole situation was anomalous. Theoretically Edward possessed the plenitude of kingship; actually he did as he was told, though all the acts of the Protector and the Council were performed in the King's name and drew their validity from him. This meant either government by a committee or by a Protector who, without being royal, could comport himself as though he were a king. The Duke of Somerset often showed himself highly dictatorial, much to the distaste of the Councilors whom he did not hesitate to put down with a high hand. This greatly contributed to his undoing, though the Council got a much more ruthless tyrant in his place.

For some time religion was left undisturbed. Yet, ominous signs appeared almost at once, indicating that a Protestant plan was ready but that it was thought advisable not to introduce it instantly. However, on December 27,* there

* December 27 was the day on which Henry died, but as his death was carefully concealed for several days, presumably the inscription on the proclamation, *"anno reg. Edward, primo,"* means it was held back until December 27, 1548. Hughes dates this as November 4, 1547, though he must have meant to write "1548." The document is contained in Strype, Vol. II, Part II, in an appendix, pp. 340–43. There those are condemned who speak irreverently against the Sacrament of the Altar, which is declared to be Christ's Body and Blood, though without precise definition; and nobody is to "revile, . . . or despise the said Sacrament, by calling it an *idol.*" All that is of course perfectly Henrician—one might even say Catholic. But there are also these words, "the holy

was issued a proclamation containing words that show that Somerset, no doubt through Cranmer, was very cunningly trying to put Protestantism over on the English people, in direct violation of Henry VIII's will of 1546.

Nor is this all: following the vote of Convocation of 1547, Parliament voted that the marriages of clerks in Holy Orders were not null and void, and voted a still stronger measure the next year, though only a small minority of priests availed themselves of this law. And when on March 8, 1548, the *Order of the Communion* appeared and was made obligatory by Parliament, it was *not* merely a translation into English of the Communion as it is in the Latin Mass, but was modeled by Cranmer upon what the Archbishop of Cologne, who had recently gone over to Lutheranism, had devised. Yet it took in many people, as was obviously intended.*

The Mass itself was untampered with and was still to be said in Latin. But Holy Communion was itself changed—not a great deal, to be sure, though the changes introduced meant much more to a theologian than to an ordinary lay person. Everybody, however, saw at once that it was made a separate service, as though it were not an integral part

Sacrament of the body and blood of Our Lord, commonly called the *Sacrament of the Altar*." Now those words, "commonly called," appeared on the title-page of the first Book of Common Prayer, when it was issued a few months later, and the object is clear: that this was the Mass in English translation, which it certainly was not. The words were removed from the second Book of Common Prayer, which dropped the pretense not only from the title-page but from the text itself. But even the royal proclamation contained expressions, which not only are a departure from Catholic piety, but may be regarded as verging on blasphemy, the very thing the proclamation purports to reprehend.

* Philip Hughes, *The Reformation in England,* Vol. II, pp. 101–102, 115.

of the Mass. This made it much easier to explain in a non-Catholic sense the Body and Blood of Christ. The move was exceedingly artful but shows that the new governors of England—and Cranmer was their theological agent, if not one of the prime movers himself—were feeling their way, not sure how far they dared go in an England which on this point at least was orthodox. This new *Order of the Communion* was fastened as a legal obligation on all priests on Easter Sunday, which fell in 1548 on April 1st.

This was merely the start. On July 9, 1549, Whitsunday, the first Book of Common Prayer was made obligatory by Parliament, and as several bishops refused to accept it, they were, after some controversy with Cranmer, imprisoned and remained imprisoned for the rest of Edward's reign. It was given out officially that Gardiner, at the Fleet—later he was sent to the Tower—"lived as much at his ease as he had been in his own house," but Gardiner's own account of the matter was rather different, for he said he had a dark room in what was called the King's Tower and that he was not permitted to have any exercise, much the same being true of Bonner. Probably none of these men was treated like other prisoners; at all events in the Tower Gardiner got along fairly well, for there he managed to write six books, compile an anthology of Latin verse, and compose some Latin verse of his own. He also sedulously pursued Cranmer when his views became more definitely Protestant. It may be that he was even too forceful a controversialist, for he pounced on the subtitle of the Book of Common Prayer— "Commonly called the Mass"—to show how very different it really was from the Mass.

However, Gardiner was not the main person who cried out against the second Book of Common Prayer, that of

1552. The first edition of that work was severely criticized by Protestants on the Continent, on the ground that it did not go nearly far enough, and as droves of foreign theological experts began to arrive in England—men who knew much more than Cranmer ever did—they were at hand to advise him about almost every sentence he wrote. The wonder is that the Prayer Book of 1552 is as moderate—and as English in tone—as it is. Cranmer at least deserves a good deal of credit for what he managed to do with heretical ideas which we know he derived from his advisers, men of varied and often rather extreme ideas.

There is this much to be said for the production in English of such a book as Cranmer compiled. Mass in the first Christian centuries was said everywhere in the vernacular—which was usually Greek—until about the fourth century, when it was said in Latin, not in Rome but in North Africa. Moreover, at the present moment there are about twenty vernacular usages which are retained by small groups —and some that are not very small—or by the Churches of what are called the Eastern Rites, all carefully protected by the Holy See.* Usually, but not invariably, these Churches of the Eastern Rites administer Holy Communion in both kinds. And many of them have married priests—that is, priests who married before receiving the diaconate. They are to be found here and there even in America, and in greater numbers than is generally imagined. There is nothing the least un-Catholic in a vernacular Mass, though for English-speaking Catholics Mass is always said in Latin. And Cranmer may have honestly believed that he was returning

* I am not referring to the Greek and Orthodox Churches, which are of course large and schismatical. The reference is to their Catholic counterparts, for fragments of them have returned to the Roman obedience and there are some who claim never to have left it.

166

to Catholic usage in encouraging frequent Communion. This would have been the case, had a law not been introduced that *forced* at least one member of every family to communicate every Sunday. Encouragement would have left a laudable action voluntary, as it should be; to make it compulsory under Parliamentary law is something quite different. One can only conclude that Cranmer was a bit hazy about Christian antiquity.

The overwhelming mass of the English people naturally resented being driven to the Communion rail by act of Parliament, especially by the changes that were introduced even before the Book of Common Prayer appeared. Here we may see the first step taken against the Mass, even though the Mass itself was left intact until 1549. Yet it is possible that there was no definite plan at first, merely improvisation which gradually grew harder and more definite under the pressure of learned foreign heretics. Pollard quotes an unnamed wit who (without assenting to the proposition) said some people almost argue that the Church of England was Protestant up to the time of the Reformation and became Catholic afterwards. One knows what is meant by that: early English Catholicism was relatively easy-going, and under the impact of events after the sixteenth century tightened up its doctrinal definition, whereas High Church Anglicanism (though it never became general) soon appeared and tried to represent itself as the norm. Like similar sallies, this one contains a grain of truth, but only a grain. In any broad sense the witticism is demonstrably untrue. Certainly the two successive Edwardian regimes set out to make England Protestant in a way that must have made old Henry VIII —a devout Catholic of the anti-Papal variety—turn over in his grave at Windsor.

Chapter Fourteen

The First Book of Common Prayer

The Duke of Somerset remains a good deal of a puzzle. It is not hard to understand why to the peasantry of England he was known as the "Good Duke," for they condoned much (and saw little else) because he opposed the enclosure movement which had been going on since the days of Henry VII. Otherwise he was rapacious and dictatorial. Cardinal Wolsey had taken something of the same line, probably because of what Sir Thomas More had written in the *Utopia*. But it is hard to believe that the man who introduced the Chantries Act had the idealism with which Pollard credits him, or that the man who demolished London churches to obtain material for the building of his palace was anything but rapacious. The best that can be said of him was that he was not so bad as the Duke of Northumberland who ousted him.

Yet the abortive campaign against Scotland, which opened almost as soon as Edward ascended the throne in 1547, may be considered statesmanlike in its inception. The Scottish Tudors naturally were not ingratiated by the fact that the descendants of Henry VIII's sister Margaret, were excluded from the royal succession, for if Mary and Elizabeth were really illegitimate, the little Queen of Scots, at this time a child of five, should have come after Edward, if he died without issue. Yet the Scots preferred their close alliance with the French, and preferred it all the more after Cardinal Beaton had been got rid of by murder because he was so strong an upholder of Scottish nationalism. Henry VIII accomplished nothing by attacking Scotland in 1542; neither did Somerset six years later, except that the lands South of the Forth were devastated, and that Mary was sent to France for safe keeping.

Yet Somerset's professed aims, as put into the proclamation he distributed in Scotland, were full of sweetness and light. That his method of trying to give them effect was bad and brought on his head the charge of hypocrisy does not alter the fact that the aims themselves were good. They were brought into being with James I and endure to this day, as they are sure to endure in any future than can be foreseen.

This was the union of the two kingdoms, and the obvious way of effecting it most easily was by the marriage of the cousins Edward and Mary, or rather by a treaty which should guarantee this marriage as soon as the children were old enough. But the Scots were afraid this would mean that their country would be absorbed by the larger, richer, and more powerful England and that they would do better to preserve their independence, which could best be done by maintaining the traditional alliance with France. That there were some disadvantages in this was admitted: if England went to war with France, Scotland might be dragged in, but that danger was remote, since England would not wish to take on two enemies at the same time. Much more common were border raids, but from these Scotland derived more benefit than England, and the raids could always be called unauthorized. But this time the war was disastrous to Somerset's political fortunes, for he was not particularly good as a military commander, whereas John Dudley (or the Earl of Warwick, as he was then) demonstrated his ability at the bloody battle of Pinkie, and this very much raised his prestige.

Moreover, immediately after his return to England, he had a further opportunity for raising his prestige in the same way. Robert Kett and his brother, men of some substance, put themselves at the head of 30,000 others in Norfolk. In the West of England and in the Thames valley, the risings were mainly by way of protest against the introduction of the first Book of Common Prayer, but in Norfolk the main motive was economic. Kett and his followers were offered a pardon if they would disperse, but this was rejected on the grounds that, since they had committed no offense, they sought no pardon. Warwick understood how to deal with that situation, and moving at once with a well-trained force, at the battle of Dusindale butchered 3,000 poorly armed (or even unarmed) rustics, afterwards doing summary execution.

Slightly earlier there had been uprisings on account of the Book of Common Prayer. In the Thames valley these were scattered and were easily put down, many priests being hanged from their own steeples as a warning not to continue saying the Mass in Latin. The uprisings in the West of England—Devonshire and more particularly Cornwall—were more serious. The rebels demanded that the Act of Six Articles, which had been very popular, should be revived; that Cardinal Pole be brought home and given a seat in the Council; that in every county two abbeys be refounded; but especially that the Latin Mass be restored with Holy Communion in only one kind for the laity. From this

it is evident that much more than Henricianism was wanted
—though that had been tolerated—and that a reunion with
Rome was the object now. The Pilgrimage of Grace had
already made this clear; twelve years later we see the eastern counties asking for virtually the same things. Much had
been put up with out of fear of the old King's ferocity;
England had no wish to put up with something much worse,
just because Somerset and Cranmer clearly intended to carry
the Reformation to still greater lengths.

The Cornishmen had a special grievance; in that county
Cornish was still spoken and English was not understood by
many people, though all were able to follow the Latin Mass
because they were familiar with the ritual. These rebels,
however, were not well armed, whereas the mercenaries—
Germans, Swiss and Italians—used in the war against Scotland had not yet gone home.* Against them the western
forces were not able to stand. One is chilled to hear of some
of the things the royal army did. Thus, Sir Anthony Kingston, son of the Kingston who had been Constable of the
Tower, descended upon Bodmin and invited himself to dinner at the house of the Mayor, Henry Braye. After dinner
he enquired casually of his host whether there were strong

---

* Many of the professional soldiers were Catholics, but did not let
that interfere with what they were called upon to do. They were led
by Lord Russell, who had been a Catholic up to this time, but
he knew where his interests lay, as he had obtained the property of
the attainted Marquis of Exeter in 1539, as well as thirty expropriated monastic manors. He later obtained others, including the great
prize of Woburn Abbey, which became the seat of the Dukes of Bed-
ford. As might be expected of such a man, he turned coat upon Queen
Mary's accession, as did also Lord Grey de Wilton. This man, after
defeating the rebels at Clyst Heath, made a general massacre of his
prisoners, but he was to show himself a brave soldier at the defense
of Calais.

gallows in the town. When assured that there were Kingston suggested that they go and inspect them. Yes, they were
strong enough: "Then up you go," he said to Braye, "for
they are for you. There is no remedy; up you go!" And
the Mayor was hanged without trial, under martial law.

Cranmer in 1550 preached a long sermon against the western rebels, and in 1549 he answered their manifesto, point
by point, to his own satisfaction, if not theirs.* The gist of
his remarks may be found in the sentence, "How an absolute Papist varieth from a heretic or traitor, I know not;
but that a Papist is both a heretic and a traitor withal."
There he showed his hand plainly. He also tossed overboard his great friend Henry VIII, for whom in unassuag-
able grief he now wore a beard, writing that the Councils
of the Church "vary so much from the Six Articles, that
either you must put the General Councils of the Church
out of your book, or else the Six Articles." We need not
dwell on his saying that Christ ordained both the kinds, as
well for laymen as for priests, "and that to be eaten and
drunken at all times." That is merely a matter of Catholic
discipline for the Western Church and is not the *doctrine*
of the Church Universal. But now Cranmer shows a bitter-
ness and coarseness unusual with him in saying, "Oh! superstition and idolatry, how they prevail among you. . . .
You will eat often of the unsavory and poisoned bread † of
the Bishop of Rome, and drink of his stinking puddles,

* *Miscellaneous Writings and Letters of Thomas Cranmer,* pp. 163–
187.

† This "holy bread" of course was the same thing as the *pain bènit,*
distributed to this day in Churches in France. Cranmer must have
known very well that it was only what is called a "sacramental," not
a sacrament, for it is handed around in baskets.

which he nameth holy bread and holy water." He rejects Purgatory, again denying what was dear to his beloved Henry VIII. As for Cardinal Pole, he is neither worthy to dwell in this realm, "nor yet to live." He even condemns the rebels wholesale to hell, telling them, "If the whole world should pray for you until doomsday, their prayers should no more avail for you than they should avail the devils in hell, unless you be penitent and sorry for your disobedience."

Some extenuation may be allowed for Cranmer on the ground that he thought this was the only kind of language these people would understand, but it is painful to find such words coming from a man of his refinement. They make unmistakably clear that he has dropped his Henrician Catholicism, though we might be unjust to regard that as having been no more than subservience to the old King, for his thought was even now in process of development.

The extremists, both on the Continent and in England, were far from satisfied with the first Book of Common Prayer. However, their objections were often wide of the mark; Cranmer thought of himself as producing a liturgy, where they demanded a creed. And it must be said that while virtually all of the Protestant creeds of this time have been discarded, or modified almost beyond recognition, Cranmer's Prayer Book has endured largely because it sought to avoid controversy or definite statement. Especially when we remember how fierce religious controversy was in those days, we shall see how irenic by comparison was Cranmer's intention. It was not the Mass in English translation, but it contained enough of the prayers that were taken from the Missal for some people to accept it as the

Latin Mass in an English dress. Most of all it beguiled by its exquisite literary charm.

Upon its first introduction there were priests who tried to make it seem like the Mass by using as many as possible of the old ceremonial gestures, or by so mumbling the words that one could hardly tell whether they were Latin or English. Some such priests may even have actually been saying Mass, behind a shield of unintelligibility, as it were. More of them probably deliberately mumbled the English words so as to deceive their flocks into believing that they were using Latin. The whole situation remained a bit confused until well into the reign of Elizabeth; for even those who were well aware that the Book of Common Prayer was being used, in some instances continued to attend the Anglican services, calling it "bowing in the house of Rimmon," arriving late, parading their inattentiveness, leaving as early as they could, and ridiculing the minister afterwards. Such practices, though not general, were finally stopped by severe action on the part of Pope Pius V. The difficulties of the imprisoned Mary Queen of Scots were such that some of the gentlemen of her household would sometimes go, for the sake of appearances, to the parish church, which observed the Elizabethan ritual, afterwards (or first) attending the Latin Mass said by one of Mary's chaplains. There were even a few priests who attempted the compromise of using the Prayer Book officially and of privately saying a Latin Mass for Catholics.

However, all this brings us down a little too far in time; the western rustics who made their vehement protest against the Book of Common Prayer did not think of such ingenious subterfuges, and well it was for the good of their souls that they did not. They saw in their simplicity that what they were being offered—at the point of a spear in 1549—was *not* the Mass, and it was the Mass that they wanted, not English prose, whose beauty they could not begin to appreciate, and which in any event was not the Holy Sacrifice.

The second Book of Common Prayer, published in 1552, was not issued as an improvement upon the literary quality of the first, even though here and there Cranmer touched up slightly that aspect of his work. It was intended merely to advance the Protestant cause. But this much may be said of both versions: that where translations of the ancient prayers of the Catholic Church were used, the translation was often an improvement upon the original—if literary art alone be considered—grand though the originals were.

Cranmer's other writing does not have this quality, being usually verbose, though it has clarity enough to convey his meaning, and that alone is a good thing to be able to say of any kind of writing. But his Book of Common Prayer, like his litany, stands apart in a completely different class. At the time, people did not realize how great writing of this sort is or appreciate at their true worth what everybody—whether Catholic or Protestant—cannot but admire. Yet even this does not quite accurately state the matter, for no doubt there are thousands—perhaps millions—without enough education to make a due evaluation, who nevertheless have been insensibly but most deeply affected by what Cranmer produced. One does not need to be a literary critic, able to explain why or precisely how one is impressed by beauty, to make a response to it, especially if by the repetition of it a quiet saturation of the mind is achieved.

But it must be added that minds of another type, who perhaps would gladly enter the Roman fold, are so spellbound and enchanted by what Cranmer provided in his Book of Common Prayer that they find it almost impossible to renounce it.* Those who have the courage to do so, will probably find that the *corpus* of the Latin Liturgy is adequate compensation for anything that they give up, as, of course, they will find the Catholic Faith gives an inexhaustible richness to their lives.

Much less successful than this was the idea he conceived, or had suggested to him, of gathering a Council of the Church—that is, of the various Reformers—which would not only be independent of Trent but perhaps obtain an authority similar to Rome's. The idea, of course, was that of reconciling divergent views, but it was a fanciful idea, as Cranmer should have discovered in somewhat similar conferences in 1538 between English and Lutheran theologians. That was mainly Cromwell's project, but it reveals something that seems rather pleasant in Cranmer's incurably sanguine character.

* Of course it is not only Cranmer who has woven the bonds that hold them. One cannot but grant that English literature is, as Cardinal Newman was to say, almost entirely a Protestant literature. There is nothing, so far as I know, that would prevent a Catholic from reading and rejoicing in such writers as Andrewes and Donne, but the fact that they are Anglican writers, holds many people out of the Church. Even for the reading of the Authorized version, normally the permission of one's Ordinary is expected, more on account of the notes that are usually appended than because of anything very injurious to Faith in the text. Yet there can be no question that the Authorized version is, considered solely as literature, the grandest of all versions, and the one that, even more than the Book of Common Prayer, is the greatest thing of its kind that ever happened. However, we are concerned only with what Cranmer did, and that is beyond praise. It

Sanguine, yes; but realistic, no. If he knew much theology, he must have been aware, that the only power qualified to summon such a Council was the Pope, and as the Pope had been pitched overboard, at least the Emperor should have been consulted, or (for a council in England) at the very least, the King. Perhaps Cranmer did mention the matter to the boy-King, Edward VI. Yet he thought of this Council as something not merely for England but for those Reformers who had broken with the Catholic Church and whose varieties of opinions could, in a consultative assembly, perhaps, somehow reach unity of doctrine. Similarly Cranmer hoped that the liturgy he had devised would be accepted everywhere, of which, it need hardly be said, there was not the remotest chance. Yet it seemed possible that such a Council and liturgy, though completely *ultra vires,* would force the hand of the Pope—though nobody had any precise idea in what direction the Reformed Catholic Church was likely to go. The whole scheme was vague and chimerical, though it produced some syncretism in England.

Poor little King Edward, of course, had no clear concepts of this kind but gave (or Protector Somerset gave) a general approval. The Council never did meet, and the disunited Reformers advocated notions that could only make them all the more disunited. Many of the Reformers wished to carry the Reformation much further than Cranmer intended to go. Yet Cranmer prepared a curious revision of the Breviary, which, as we know from the bits that have come down to us, was to be said in Latin. Nothing came of this revision, even in England. It reveals that a regrouping of

will be grasped, let us hope, that nothing is being spoken of except literary merits. Even Mr. Belloc has nothing but good to say of Cranmer in this way, unfair as he seems to me in other respects.

the Psalms was suggested—to which, in principle, the Holy See might not have objected, and indeed Cranmer was greatly influenced by the revisions proposed with an irenical intention by the Spanish Franciscan Cardinal, Quignon. But of course Cranmer went much further than Quignon, throwing out many of the divisions of the Breviary. Cranmer was very drastic, even while retaining—though for Vespers!—the great hymn for Compline, *Te lucis ante terminum*.

As for the commemoration of the saints, those most honored by the Church were thrown out wholesale. In their place Cranmer proposed the names of Biblical characters —mostly from the Old Testament—but he would not have found much enthusiasm, even among the Reformers, for bringing in Jonah, Amos, Daniel, Judith, Job, and similar personages.* That enterprise of Cranmer's was almost fantastically abortive.

Even the literary merits of the Book of Common Prayer, which were totally ignored by foreign Protestants, were only slowly recognized in England. Yet so little doctrine was explicitly stated, though much was implied, that the Forty-two Articles—reduced to Thirty-nine during the reign of Elizabeth—had to be drawn up to set forth the official position of the Anglican Church. It is notorious that many sign the Articles today with tongue in cheek.

For this document, the learned Protestant theologians from abroad were largely responsible. Of those who came to England to subject Cranmer to a kind of brain-washing, the German Martin Bucer was the most influential. Perhaps the most brilliant of the lot was Bernardino Ochino, the

---

* Cranmer's whole scheme is minutely examined by J. Wickham Legg in his *Cranmer's Liturgical Projects,* London, 1915.

former General of the Capuchins, but as he was an orator rather than a theologian, he was more decorative than useful. Eventually he destroyed his standing even among Protestants by advocating what everybody had to admit was highly heretical—polygamy, for instance.

We think of the Book of Common Prayer as being very "English" in tone, yet it was produced largely under the direction of foreign scholars. Cranmer's magnificent prose style permeates everything, so that, while its origins are foreign and synthetic, the final result is characteristically English. For this Cranmer has to be thanked. Nevertheless it should not be forgotten that he needed the aid of learned foreign heretics. Whatever might be his deficiencies in political sagacity (or even theological learning) his literary taste was not in the least affected by the suggestions of the advisers he had imported from abroad. Perhaps he was saved by the fact that they knew little or no English.

Chapter Fifteen

England Under a New Master

The appearance of a second Book of Common Prayer in 1552 had little or nothing to do with the fact that John Dudley, the Earl of Warwick, displaced the Duke of Somerset as the acting head of the state. It was not produced at the instance of the Duke of Northumberland, as Warwick soon styled himself. Indeed, the first Prayer Book was of a somewhat tentative nature, especially since it was severely criticized by some of the foreign theologians and the more extreme Protestants in England. Still, the revision bears upon every page the stamp of Cranmer, who managed to give the work a seemly and moderate character, while being always definitely Protestant.

But while Cranmer had tried in 1549 to avoid doctrinal statements, especially regarding the Sacrament of the Altar, doctrine was implied in almost every line. Bishop Gardiner was relentless in charging him with heresy, and continued to pursue him through all the winds of doctrine blowing from Northern Europe. Even when Cranmer issued one of his controversial works anonymously, in order to escape such criticism, Gardiner used the infuriating device of affecting to believe that the book could not be Cranmer's because its Protestantism was so pronounced. By referring to "this author," as though he were some well masked man, he incensed the Archbishop very highly, because Gardiner understood perfectly who the real author was, and Cranmer knew just as perfectly that he did.

Yet there were factors in the case that may have escaped the shrewd Bishop of Winchester. Cranmer's theological ideas were in process of development as a consequence of the many foreign scholars (all more or less heretical) he had invited to England, giving them hospitality—sometimes for months—before he was able to secure them professorships at the universities, or some other good benefices. Under their guidance he was steadily reading, just as he had read a great deal while still a Cambridge Don, and though he cannot be considered a notable thinker, or much more than the expounder of other men's ideas, he was a very different man from what he had been while Henry VIII was on the throne, or even from the Cranmer at the beginning of Edward's reign.

From abroad there came into England some of the heretics for whom other countries had become too hot. Bernardino Ochino, who was one of them, was not a great scholar but he was a great orator and had actually been General of the newly founded Capuchins, a reformed branch of the Franciscans, when his long-suspected heresy eventually became all too apparent, causing him to withdraw in a hurry. It was different with the aristocratic Pole, John à Lasco. As he had been offered a bishopric in his native land, his declared Protestantism must have been sincere. Nor is there any reason to doubt the genuineness of men like the German, Martin Bucer, who was perhaps more influential with Cranmer than anybody else, or Peter Martyr Vermigli, an ex-Augustinian, who was appointed Regius Professor at Oxford, or the Jewish Tremellino. This last was a curious case, for Cardinal Pole had first made him a Catholic, and then Ochino had seduced him. As a distinguished Hebrew scholar, he found an appointment at Cambridge. There were many others, especially those who took charge of the churches for foreigners, but they are too numerous to mention, and not so learned as the men listed.

It was men of this type whom Cranmer hoped to organize into a reforming Church Council, without any success, and indeed without having anything remotely resembling the authority for doing so. There is a possibility, however, that some such assembly could have been used to give an appearance of unity to the disparate groups of Protestants had only some other indispensable figures consented to come to England, but there seemed no chance of bringing this about. The celebrated Calvin was definitely hostile, for he had come to consider himself as a kind of Pope; as such, he rigidly excluded all beliefs that did not exactly coincide with his own, and he had the justification that the clarity of his French mind and the clarity of expression found in his *Institutes* gave him at that time an advantage over all other heresiarchs, for he provided a complete (if narrow) system, and a definite discipline.* The almost equally celebrated Lutheran, Philip Melanchthon, though pressed over and over again by Cranmer to come, never did. He expressed sympathy with the project of a Council, but he invariably found some reason for declining; usually it was his health or his age (he was fifty) or the discomfort or danger of a

---

* This advantage has long since been lost; it would be very hard to find any thoroughgoing Calvinists today, though of course Calvin has influenced most modern Protestant bodies to a greater or lesser extent.

sea voyage—always something. His real reason, however, was in all probability his disillusionment about the possibility of a united stand among Reformers. This had been attempted and had failed in 1538, and as Melanchthon at that time had authorized the making of many concessions, only to see his sweet reasonableness rebuffed by Henry VIII, he had come to regard unity as unobtainable, and was sure that Lutherans, Zwinglians and Calvinists would never agree. In the end Melanchthon simply would not answer Cranmer's letters.

The foreign churches in England presented something of a problem. Nicholas Ridley who, after having been Bishop of Rochester in 1547, had been translated to London, did not at all like it that groups of Italians and Flemings and Germans should be permitted the use of their own conventicles and their own liturgy. He believed that they should use the Book of Common Prayer and that, if necessary, translations of it should be made for them. They were an anomaly, and yet their independence was protected. They did, after all, give a more definite tone to England's new religion; this was all to the good, as it was very evident that many—indeed most—people were Catholic in sympathy.

It is only just to Cranmer to remark that, while he may not have taken any lead in educational matters—his time being usually taken up in other matters—he did not forget that there was great need for education. Like other Protestant leaders he deplored the fact that the two English universities had suffered a great deal from the Reformation, but, like other people, he hoped that such a serious state of affairs would prove only temporary, as, in fact, was the case. Even so, the Reformation changed the character of the universities considerably. They had been, of a sort, seminaries for the priesthood, which almost anybody could find the means to attend, and the Reformation changed them to clubs for rich and usually idle young men. When the pillaging of the monasteries occurred, the Archbishop managed to get the monks of the Cathedral priory at Canterbury transformed into prebendaries, canons and the like. As for the school under their charge, when some suggested that it be reserved for gentlemen's sons, as otherwise it would become hard to find men to till the soil, Cranmer nobly answered the objections. It was to the effect that while admittedly we do need laborers and farmhands, the sons of fathers of lowly station are often richly endowed in mental gifts. He did not argue that only such students should be admitted, but merely that they should not be excluded. Otherwise, it would mean a human decision that the lowly "were unworthy to have the gifts of the Holy Ghost bestowed upon them . . . that Almighty God should not be at liberty to bestow His great gifts of grace upon any person." As for the sons of the well born, Cranmer said that often they "were most unapt to learn and very dolts, as I myself have seen no small number of them very dull and without any manner of capacity." * This was written about the time of Cromwell's downfall in 1540, and Cranmer may have had in mind Cromwell's son Gregory as being of this stamp. He later tried to protect poor students, when, during the reign of Edward VI, there was a pillaging of most things available to the rich, but then he found himself unable to do much against the rapacity of those governing in the name of the boy king.

During the regime (or dictatorship) of Northumberland, there appeared a radical Puritanism with which Cranmer

* Strype, *Memorials of Thomas Cranmer* (Oxford, 1848–54), Vol. I, pp. 127–28.

was out of sympathy. Among its leaders was John Hooper, who became Bishop of Gloucester and Worcester, and who was burned at the stake in 1555. Hooper wished to divest the Church of England of everything that suggested its former connection with Rome. There were no longer to be altars but tables, and these were usually placed endwise in the sanctuary, while the altars were used as flagstone entrances into the church. There was also a good deal of acrimonious controversy over the posture in which Communion was to be received, and as kneeling suggested the adoration of the Host (which was regarded as idolatrous), standing or sitting was preferred.* But somebody sarcastically pointed out that if the mode used in the Last Supper were strictly followed, the communicants should recline on couches.

Most of all Hooper objected to what he called the priest's "Aaronical" vestments. He made himself such a nuisance over this that Northumberland clapped him into the Tower, because, when nominated a bishop, Hooper resolutely declined to wear any vestments, least of all those of a bishop —and this though Northumberland was Hooper's main ally in most matters. In the end a compromise was reached: Hooper would dress like a bishop upon a few special occasions, so long as at other times he was permitted to dress as he liked. Even some of the foreign theologians—who were generally inclined to take an extreme position—told Hooper that he was making a fuss about a point of little importance.

* In some of the Churches of the Eastern Rite under the jurisdiction of Rome, Holy Communion is received standing. In some modern nonconformist bodies sitting is almost universal. But I understand that in the *Ecclesia Anglicana* there is now no question as to the propriety of kneeling.

Northumberland was very devious in his methods. He began to build up an opposition to Protector Somerset, and soon greatly added to his prestige by proving himself an excellent military commander in his victory at Pinkie, during the war with Scotland, and again in 1549 by his bloody suppression of the Norfolk rebels at Dusindale. Even so, he realized that Somerset, being entrenched in power, might be hard to overthrow. He therefore gave it out among the more Catholic-minded members of the Council that he planned a Catholic reaction, and by this device contrived to detach some of the politicians from Somerset.

The trick worked; he did receive a strong Catholic backing; and when he had succeeded in pulling down the Protector, there was great rejoicing among many people. In some places the Book of Common Prayer, though imposed by statute, was discarded by the priests, who reverted to saying the old Latin Mass. Yet when Northumberland had got the reins of government safely into his hands, he pursued an even more radically Protestant policy than Somerset. What the man's real religious opinions were is a question. The day before he was executed, after the accession of Queen Mary in 1553, he made the most public profession of Catholicism, but Lady Jane Grey, that daughter-in-law of his whom he had briefly made a queen, declared that all this was only a pretense. However, she hated him and had a notoriously sharp tongue and cannot be considered a very reliable witness. Cranmer, for his part, may have feared that Northumberland's coming into power really did mean that all his own work would be undone. But in this the Archbishop showed himself out of touch with political realities, as usual with him. The new regime sought support from the extremists, of whom Cranmer did not quite

approve, and Cranmer's position was now made rather difficult because moderate Protestantism was being almost swept
away by the class of men whom Hooper represented.

The Duke of Northumberland—for that was the title the
Earl of Warwick conferred upon himself, making the Marquis of Dorest Duke of Suffolk—did not style himself Protector, though he acted with an even higher hand than had
the fallen Somerset, but was ostensibly on an equality with
the other members of the Council. With the extremists
among the Protestants he made a kind of bargain, as when
he offered John Knox a bishopric (which, however, the
canny Scot declined, though he accepted a pension). The
understanding reached with men like Hooper was that he
was to be given full rein, on condition that no obstacle be
put in the way of his own looting of bishoprics. Some bishoprics were even suppressed, as was that of Westminster,
founded by Henry VIII, and its revenues appropriated.
Gloucester was shaved close and its bishop put upon a small
salary; Winchester was plundered; and Durham—a very rich
prize—Northumberland intended to pocket, adding the diocesan holdings to those of his duchy. Tunstall's revenues
were not, however, to be seized *in toto;* the Duke merely
intended to take the greater part and, with what little remained, endow two unimportant bishoprics in the North of
England.

Cranmer deplored such spoliation. He feared that Canterbury's turn would come, but he also grieved over what other
bishoprics had to suffer, and he gazed with horror at what
was being done to parish churches that contained enough
valuables to loot. Not only were their endowments greatly
reduced, but, as Northumberland was supporting those
who wished for Puritan simplicity (of course on condition

that the support be reciprocal), their furnishings also were taken, on the ground that henceforth they would not need their plate or priceless vestments. Sometimes, even, irreplaceable stained glass was removed to give further grandeur to the houses of the rich.

If in the second Book of Common Prayer (that of 1552) there were certain touches that Cranmer indicated he did not altogether relish, this was not so much to placate Northumberland (who had little if anything to do with the matter) as to meet the criticism of more "advanced" men at home and abroad, and also because Cranmer himself was now more advanced, though he was still relatively moderate and always strove for seemliness in worship. He did not wish to antagonize Northumberland, who had it in his power to prevent the meeting of the Reformers' Council in England, of which Cranmer still dreamed. But of course, quite apart from Northumberland, there was no chance of assembling such a group. While theological discussion went on, it was conducted by small groups in an unofficial way, and though far from being ineffectual, it was hardly what Cranmer had hoped for.

Another consideration operated: Cranmer was hoping to induce Parliament to give statutory force to a revision of the Canon Law. Northumberland was not very favorable to this plan, as he was thinking of matters closer to his own interests. Yet it might have gone through Parliament except for the accession of Queen Mary. Under Cranmer's code, it is interesting to note that it would be heresy to maintain Transubstantiation. This did not necessarily mean that the "Real Absence" was to be the official doctrine, but at least the Catholic doctrine was to be made heresy, which would mean punishment by burning at the stake. The fact should be remembered when we recall Cranmer's own fate.

Priests had long since been permitted to marry, and some did, though a great many more did not. Some preferred the celibacy to which they were accustomed; others believed that the sickly Edward would not live long and knew that the Catholic Mary, when she came to the throne, would be sure to deprive the married clergy of their livings. But it was soon evident that this permission to marry, far from bringing an improvement in clerical morals, was sometimes an encouragement to license. Though it may be true that Bishop Ponet, who was given the Winchester bishopric of which the imprisoned Gardiner had been deprived, really believed that his second wife's husband, a butcher in Nottingham, was dead, bigamy was in fact committed. In some cases, there is no possibility of giving any benefit of the doubt.

Thomas Cranmer drew up a doctrinal statement in the form of fifty-four articles, which have disappeared without leaving a trace. In all probability Cranmer destroyed those articles himself, when he reduced them to forty-two. It must be remembered that, no matter how glibly people have talked, Cranmer did not believe in unfettered thought. He wanted a kind of "Pickwickian" uniformity, each man being allowed some leeway of interpretation, but not too much.

Cranmer had little to do with the persecution endured by the Lady Mary, except that he had to vote, as a member of the Council, on what was being done. Mary declared that the Council had given the Emperor a promise that she should keep her Mass, but they pretended that this promise was only provisional and in the end withdrew it altogether. When the Earl of Warwick argued—logically enough—that if the Mass was of God everybody should have it, but if of the devil it should be permitted to nobody, Cranmer devised the formula that an evil thing, should the circumstances make this necessary, might be tolerated in the hope of eventual amendment. In this way Mary, under increasing pressure, held onto her Mass.

Moreover, when the Council sent a Bishop to Mary to try to show her the error of her ways, it was not Cranmer but Ridley who was sent. And Mary told Ridley quite bluntly where she stood; she was determined not to yield an inch. The Archbishop took good care to keep out of the way of so forthright a woman, not one who could be wheedled or cajoled, and who, he feared, had a grudge against him because he had arranged the divorce of Henry from her mother. There was, in fact, no such grudge, but Cranmer—a man always inclined to be timid—was right in believing that he was not the type to deal with Mary. Nicholas Ridley, as we have said, was the one who went to her. His encounter with the Lady Mary was of course only an incident in his career. What is more important is that he was the fellow-countryman upon whom Cranmer leaned most, for he had greater learning than the other new bishops—no doubt because of having studied at the Sorbonne and Louvain. Though rather more "advanced" than Cranmer, he was still more or less a middle-of-the-road man. Many thought (perhaps correctly) that he, rather than the German Bucer, had had most to do with the development of Cranmer's thought. Indeed, Cranmer himself sometimes gave Ridley rather than Bucer the credit for bringing him to a position which, with timid steps and slow, it took him about twenty years to reach.

Being what he was, Cranmer and the Duke of Northumberland were not on very good terms, the Archbishop being disgusted by the Duke's dictatorial manner and, still more, by his unabashed plundering. Perhaps the worst feature of the case was that the rapaciousness was to some extent a "deal" with the religious extremists, whom the Duke appointed to good benefices as soon as they became available. It even had much of the color of simony, as the good appointments always went to those willing to allow the Duke or his chief supporters to scoop up a large part of ecclesiastical revenues.

After Protector Somerset's fall at the beginning of 1550 he was imprisoned in the Tower for about a month but was then readmitted to the Council, though without his former authority. No charges had been preferred at that time, for there had been nothing in his policy that could be considered criminal except that, like the rest of the politicians, he had been greedy. When he returned to the Council, Somerset began to look for some means of returning to power, so in the following year he was rearrested—this time on a completely bogus charge of treason. As became evident at his trial, no treason could be proved; the charge was quickly changed to that of felony—which also was punishable by death. When the crowds saw him emerge from Westminster Hall with the guards' axes turned away from him they supposed that his acquittal had been complete. It was not so; Northumberland had determined that his rival must die, and therefore he was led out to the block—very early in the morning, so that there would be few people on Tower Hill.* Even so, rumours of what was

* This of course was merely judicial murder, the approved way, during this period, of disposing of a discredited politician. Somerset deserves no sympathy, yet, of course, he had been unjustly treated and was paying the penalty for rapacity and high-handedness.

191

about to happen spread quickly, and a crowd gathered. First, a horseman rode up as though he carried a last-minute pardon, and this caused delay. Then there was a commotion caused by the firing of a gun. Somerset, if he had been a more daring character, could easily have leaped from the scaffold. To many people he was the "Good Duke" still, and he would have been hidden, with a good chance of being smuggled out of England. Instead he stood irresolute; then he laid his head on the block and had it cut off.

So passed Cranmer's chief collaborator during the reign of Edward VI. But he had the satisfaction of knowing, with the publication of the Second Book of Common Prayer in 1552, that his work had been accomplished. He had long since given up his fantastic dream of a Council of the Church in England, and while he would have liked to see his new code of Canon Law accepted by Parliament, even he must have realized—though his hold upon realities was slight— that it would not have lasted long, even had Mary never become Queen. The code was too ferocious, and such ferocity, eventually and inevitably, faded from Protestantism. But his Book of Common Prayer has molded the mind of England. This is an extraordinary instance of the sheer power of style.

In the Spring of 1553 Northumberland devised his famous plot. It is not necessary here to go into all the details of the series of marriages that were contracted to strengthen Northumberland's position. The main thing is that Henry VIII's will was to be disregarded, as he had named his daughters Mary and Elizabeth (though legally illegitimate) to succeed Edward. As Edward was each day drawing closer to death, Lady Jane Grey was to be proclaimed Queen. Since Northumberland had married her to his son, Lord Guildford

Dudley, he himself counted upon being the power behind the throne.

The Duke could not have known much about the character of his young daughter-in-law. Because she was prim, he seems to have imagined her demure and placable, whereas she had a tart tongue and a will of her own. Had she succeeded in maintaining herself as Queen, she would have ruled decisively and put Northumberland in his place. Even if the Duke had any inkling of the fact that Jane was not the gentle dove he supposed, he still believed that he could force her to obey him. Confident of this, he sent an army to the Isle of Wight, in case the French should invade; he had ships held in readiness in the Thames; he mounted guns on the Tower and raised train-bands; finally, he withheld payment of every possible debt, while dunning all the Crown's debtors. One must admit that the man took every possible precaution. The only trouble was that he had not accurately gauged the feeling of England, its attachment to the Tudors, and its hatred of himself.

Cranmer, one would suppose, must have heard some account of what was going on, but, as he seldom attended the Council, he may not have been given full details until he was asked to witness the will of the dying young King. Then he demurred. In the first place, had the boy any right to make a will bequeathing the Crown? Henry VIII had done so, setting a doubtful and dangerous precedent, but the old King had been empowered to act so by Parliament. Now Cranmer, together with the leading politicians, had sworn to uphold that will. Though he could at other times perjure himself, this was a time when he felt a sudden scruple. He had not hesitated to set aside Henry's order that there should be no changes in religion until his son was twenty-four, but for that there was intervention by Parliament. Cranmer felt that the succession was a weightier matter. Moreover, he did not wish to support Lady Jane Grey.

For this, Thomas Cranmer deserves a great deal of credit, since the alternative was the Lady Mary, and her accession, as he knew, would mean a return to the Roman obedience, or at least to the Henrician form of Catholicism. Then the Latin Mass would come back and the Book of Common Prayer be discarded. It could even mean that Cranmer would be forced to resign his archbishopric. The course of Protestantism in England would end abruptly. For this reason, there were some who—not particularly enthusiastic about Jane, concerning whom they knew little, and anything but enthusiastic about Northumberland, about whom they knew too much—felt that Jane had to be backed, which was an argument that the Duke used for all it was worth.

The judges also objected to Edward's will, when they were summoned as legal officers. Northumberland terrified them by threatening charges of treason, and as they knew that he would stick at nothing, in the end all but one of them signed. They were dealt with first, as a means of overcoming Cranmer's reluctance, for the Duke could then argue that if the judges had signed the will it was a proof that everything was legally correct. Nevertheless Cranmer tried to reason with the Duke, and as that did no good, asked that he might see the dying King. Northumberland peremptorily refused, fearing that the Archbishop might bring Edward to see that he was doing wrong. So Cranmer yielded, and if his signature appeared at the head of the proclamation of Jane as Queen, this was because he signed in the only space left. Cranmer always claimed that he was the last person to sign.* William Cecil, who had clearly seen the dangers involved, protested to Mary that he had signed only as a witness. More probably it was because his adhesion was given to the Lady Elizabeth, whom he expected to see become Queen before long, as Mary's health was not good. But a man of his acute judgment knew that England would never accept Lady Jane, especially when her father-in-law, the detested Duke, would attempt to act as the real king.

A Catholic may almost take the position of regretting that the Duke of Northumberland's plot did not succeed. This, of course, is only another instance of being wise after the event. At the time, all Catholics, without exception, rejoiced that Mary had become Queen. It was impossible for any-body to foresee the Marian persecution, which was used with such deadly effect against the Catholic Church. On the other hand, a few more years of the Duke's high-handedness (with its support of the emerging Puritans) would, so far as one can tell on the basis of theoretical logic, have made Prot-estantism in all its forms as much detested in England as was Northumberland. But this is, of course, mere specula-tion; just-minded people had no other choice except to rally around the rightful queen.

* This is mainly taken from Cranmer's own written explanations to Queen Mary, but there is no reason to suppose that he was not truth-ful.

Chapter Sixteen

Queen Mary's Triumph

Nicholas Ridley, the bishop who had been chosen by the Council to make a personal call upon the Lady Mary to persuade her of the error of her ways, was also the preacher who, at Paul's Cross, on the Sunday after Lady Jane Grey had been proclaimed Queen, argued before a large congregation that both Mary and Elizabeth, being bastards, were ineligible for the Crown. This meant that he, much more than Cranmer, who was within hand's reach at Lambeth, had completely gone over to the Duke's conspiracy. Cranmer, though he had made himself technically guilty of treason, actually had done what he could to prevent it. But he had never been a decisive man—on the contrary, usually somewhat ineffectual—and this lack in him could, in itself, have saved him from his fate, had not precisely the same thing left him at the mercy of men who knew their own minds better than was ever to be expected of him.

When it became evident that the country was going to give Queen Mary loyal support, and even Northumberland began to see that his game was up, Ridley, greatly scared on account of his sermon, went post-haste to Ipswich. There he hoped to find a ship that would carry him to some Baltic port. But when he was captured, his rather lame explanation was that he was on his way to the Queen to ask her forgiveness. Though it was not precisely like "going to Birkenhead by way of Brighton pier," it was obvious that he could have found a much quicker way to reach the Queen than by taking the road to Ipswich, despite which she accepted his protestations at their face value, and treason was not pressed against him. When two years latter he was burned at the stake, it was for the statutory offense of heresy.

Cranmer, however, had to be tried for treason, and was condemned, along with a number of other people. This was regarded as no more than a formality, for even Lady Jane's father, the Duke of Suffolk—a ring-leader in the plot —was released from the Tower after an incarceration of three days. This was because the Duchess told the Queen that her husband did not like being in prison or, as she put it, because the Tower would be bad for his health. This must have caused many who heard of it to grin broadly behind the backs of their hands, especially since Bishop Gardiner had spent six years in the Tower and the aged Duke of Norfolk seven, finding that it was a prison in which important people could have a comfortable life. But Mary was extremely kind-hearted, and it was only with the greatest reluctance that she punished anybody. She would have pardoned even Northumberland had not her advisers insisted that he be beheaded. In this, of course, they were right; the man's guilt was of so dark a character that it could not be overlooked. Besides, he was much too dangerous a person to be left at large.

Archbishop Cranmer was released in time to conduct King Edward's funeral, and he was allowed to do this according to the forms of the Book of Common Prayer, the Queen contenting herself with having a Mass said in the chapel of the Tower for the repose of her brother's soul. It must be remembered that the Act of Uniformity was still on the statute book, though its repeal was certain when

197

Parliament met. In anticipation of this, a number of priests began to say the Latin Mass again, usually much to the delight of their parishioners, though in London several unpleasant incidents occurred, fomented by the small but truculent Protestant minority there. One might almost say that, except for one or two of the East Coast towns, England had no Protestants at all.

Queen Mary had issued a proclamation that there was to be no change in religion, unless this was made when Parliament met. She was all for toleration, as all her own actions made clear. Had the good will she showed been met with a similar generosity on the part of Protestants, and especially had Wyatt's most dangerous rebellion not broken out, it is virtually certain that there would have been no religious persecution. On the contrary, Mary, in her heart, stood for a reasonableness in this matter unheard of in her day. Yet circumstances forced her to take up an attitude at variance with her own wishes, so that to the old-fashioned sort of history she is still known by the appalling title of "Bloody Mary."

Some parishes—these were in London, the center mainly infected with heresy, and a few other places—were quite undisturbed in their use of the Book of Common Prayer. But in the country parts and the university towns, the Latin Mass was restored—illegally, in the strict sense, but plainly indicating what the country wished. This does not mean that much more was expected than the Henrician mode of Catholicism, though it was taken for granted (quite correctly) that the Act of Six Articles would not be reintroduced. There were older and more moderate laws against heresy which would have amply sufficed, and everybody—Catholics and Protestants alike—were agreed that heresy was an offense, though naturally there was no uniform opinion as to what constituted heresy. The epigram coined by the eighteenth century William Warburton, Bishop of Gloucester, "Orthodoxy is my doxy, heterodoxy is your doxy," perhaps covers the point sufficiently well.

London, where most of the English Protestants were congregated, was boisterous—in fact, delirious—in its joy when Mary rode into the capital as Queen. There had never been seen so hearty and spontaneous a demonstration. Even London contained, among an estimated 100,000 inhabitants, only about 15,000 avowed Protestants, and of these about 3,000 to 5,000 were foreigners who were refugees. They were the noisiest of all the dissidents, the most bitter and the most boorish. Among Englishmen the main complaint was that the Queen had treated Northumberland and his associates too gently, for it was foreseen that this would be taken as a sign of weakness rather than of kindness. Indeed, it would have been better had Mary shown something like the usual severity at that moment, for a warning would have been issued to malcontents that they had better not try to take advantage of her.

When Mary's first Parliament assembled the Mass was restored, but no penalties were imposed upon heretics other than those which had existed for a couple of centuries, and these were relatively light. As was only to be expected, priests who had married were deprived of their benefices. But here, too, Mary was mild: a priest who had married—and such priests were only a small minority—was transferred to a part of the country where his past would be unknown. It was otherwise with the handful of married bishops: their offense could not be hidden, even if they separated from their wives, so they were deprived of their bishoprics, but could be given a benefice of a lesser sort.*

Archbishop Cranmer was not deprived of his office; he was merely not allowed to exercise it. There was a feeling in the Council that, while, of course, he could not carry on the duties of the Primate as before, he might be permitted to resign on a pension. In spite of what he had done to her mother in his court at Dunstable in 1533, Mary felt no vindictiveness towards him but probably regarded him, as did most people, as a pleasant old gentleman. She understood perfectly well that in the matter of the divorce he had merely been carrying out her father's orders, and she knew that her father was a man who would brook no disobedience.

One must give Cranmer credit for the fact that in the early months of Mary's reign he made no attempt to escape to the continent. Ridley was, as we have seen, trying to get away when caught. But Cranmer undoubtedly would have been supplied with an honorable passport to leave, had he applied for one. In this, even Stephen Gardiner, now Chancellor, would have helped, for the policy of the government was to get heretics out of England. This was true, even after the persecution began in 1555. Close to a thousand people managed to find asylum abroad, though of these perhaps the majority quietly slipped away without passports. Cranmer stayed in England, no doubt because he rightly be-

* That nothing was done to Cranmer in the matter suggests that his marriage to Osiander's niece in Nuremberg was of a private and irregular sort—in fact, something that could not be regarded as marriage, as the term was generally understood. Those who had taken advantage of the law introduced during Edward's reign, and had openly taken a wife in a church ceremony, were in a different case.

lieved that his departure would ruin the Protestant cause, and possibly because he imagined, until it was too late, that the worst that could happen to him would be the loss of his archbishopric. And, of course, he could not afford to disregard the talk of pensioning him off, a project which flight would have finished. At any rate he stayed; that he did so indicates that he had more courage than has often been supposed.

In all probability, he would, at most, have suffered house arrest in Lambeth Palace, if only he had withdrawn into the shadows and kept his mouth shut. Mary, if she did not formally pardon his treason, showed that she intended to take no action to enforce the penalty. But when rumors began to be circulated that he had said Mass for the Queen, his friend Bucer—who, being a foreigner, was in no danger —insisted that Cranmer announce that he had done nothing of the kind. Such an announcement was quite unnecessary; those in touch with the court were well aware that the rumors were baseless, as everybody would have discovered before long. This is the kind of thing that falls to the ground of its own weight, as Cranmer should have known.

Instead, he was so ill-advised as to allow an explanation to go out. This was that a man named Thornton, formerly one of the monks of the Canterbury Priory that had been attached to the cathedral and now one of his suffragan bishops, had in the Archbishop's absence permitted the Latin Mass to be said again at Canterbury. Merely to have said that and nothing else would have been permissible, but the Archbishop couched his manifesto in truculent terms and so was ordered not to leave Lambeth Palace—nothing worse.

Cranmer afterwards declared that he had written something intended only for the eyes of his friends, which was probably true; but some indiscreet person got hold of the document, with the result that it was copied and widely distributed. The Council was of the opinion that this indiscretion—it really was nothing worse—fomented the unseemly incidents that immediately followed. This may have been the case, but it is not susceptible of definite proof. We may be sure that Cranmer, great heretic though he certainly was, was just as certainly too great a gentleman to approve of incidents like the following: an ex-monk named Flowers, who had married and practiced in London as a doctor, but who seems to have been deranged, assaulted a priest who was saying Mass in the church of St. Margaret's, Westminster, stabbing him so that his blood gushed out over the Host. Also, a dagger was thrown at a Catholic preacher named Bourne in St. Paul's Cathedral; this was manifestly part of an organized demonstration on the part of fanatical ruffians, and Bourne might have been lynched had not Rogers and Bradford (both of them to be Protestant martyrs but men who did not approve of the mob's behavior) hurried him away to safety. Then a dead cat was found one morning in Chepe, hanged in priestly vestments, with its head tonsured, and with a round piece of paper representing the Blessed Sacrament between its paws. Again, a dead dog was thrown through the windows of the Council Chamber. As to the facts themselves, there is no shadow of doubt, since they are mentioned (along with the dates of the occurrences) in several contemporary chronicles, and even by John Foxe the martyrologist.

Cranmer was not only shocked by such incidents but realized how damaging they were to the Protestant cause. Other things that happened were less serious, as in the case of a girl who squeezed herself into the hollow of a wall, from which she emitted what purported to be divinations. She had to stand at Paul's Cross and confess to her hoax. So also with the youth named Fetherstone, who gave out that he was Edward VI, who had not died at all. He received a whipping—which surely he deserved—but upon a second offense he received a traitor's sentence.* Cranmer was of course in no way responsible for these things, though ignorant people may have taken his manifesto as an incitement. Loyal Englishmen, whatever their religious opinions, were incensed by these insults to the Queen. Such things had something to do with the Act of Parliament passed in 1555 calling for persecution, though of course Wyatt's rebellion was far more reprehensible, because it was far more dangerous. Wyatt had, indeed, given out that religion had nothing to do with his uprising, that it was only a protest against the Queen's projected marriage to Philip of Spain. Privately, however, he let his real objectives be known. One can only say that, deplorable though the Marian persecution was, it came only after her generous offers of good will had been most insultingly rebuffed by certain unmannerly elements (largely foreigners). The Protestants therefore had brought persecution upon their own heads. This is not to suggest that they got only what they deserved but merely that they had stretched the patience of a most kind-hearted woman beyond endurance. Even

---

* This surely was not excessive, as it was a second offense. The age was one of such impersonations, as is illustrated by Perkin Warbeck and Lambert Simnel in Henry VII's reign. Warbeck was hanged in 1499 but Simnel given no worse punishment than to be made a scullion in the royal kitchen, where no doubt he was able to get many dainty morsels of food. The early sixteenth century was a time when there was much cruelty, but also some manifestations of good-humored leniency.

the most kind-hearted of women is liable to turn suddenly angry, or even ferocious, when her affections are engaged, as Queen Mary's were with Philip.

Cranmer's manifesto marks a great change in him. His pleasant ways had got him his start, and he was still courteous and gentle. But though he may sometimes be accused of being subservient to Henry VIII, towards Queen Mary he was, if not precisely truculent, at any rate courageous—up to a point. This may have been because he knew how dangerous a man the old King was, whereas he felt that he had little to fear from this Queen, whom he had known (without ever having much to do with her) since she was a child. It may even be that the susceptible Cranmer in his heart of hearts did not have a very high opinion of women. If so, it is merely a further proof of how out of touch with realities he was.

The word "truculence" has been used for want of a better one. And there *was* something new in Cranmer, right to the end, whether one calls it rashness, courage, stubbornness, fidelity or foolishness. One cannot quite use the word "courage," though that also showed itself at last. During the last months of his life Cranmer made recantation after recantation, each a bit ampler than the one that went before, in an effort to save his own life. In trying to save it, surely he cannot be blamed, for no man ever lived who had less of what one looks for in a martyr. He was dreadfully afraid of death at the stake, and yet he wished to avoid an absolute repudiation of all that he had stood for. We shall find, I think, that every one of the recantations contained some phrase—and in the beginning much more than a single phrase—that reaffirmed his principle that the monarch had the right to say what should be believed in religion. It was all too evident that he was not submitting to the Pope at all. By some ingenious evasion, or the use of double-talk, he contrived to remain obdurate in his heresy.

But of course all this came at the end, when Cranmer went to the stake with dramatic courage because he saw that he was not going to escape. His real exhibition of cour-age—rashness, folly or what you will—was his proclamation of 1553. Yet in all probability neither he nor anybody else would have been burned had not so many heretics made themselves obnoxious, and had not Wyatt raised so dan-gerous a rebellion that his forces actually marched to the very walls of Mary's palace. She repressed this rebellion with unwonted severity, as she belatedly saw where her leniency led, and as she felt that not only she but Philip of Spain was threatened. He might even withdraw at the last moment from the projected marriage unless his alarm was allayed. The judgment of the Council was probably correct: it was the mild and accommodating Cranmer who, without intending anything of the kind, had put heart into the malcontents.

The Queen was popular—at least potentially so—both on account of what her beloved mother had suffered and be-cause of the sympathy generally extended to herself on ac-count of what she had had to suffer during Edward's reign. Even those who disagreed with her had to admire her reso-lute spirit, and those who came into personal contact with her knew she was charitable and pious and of irreproachable life. Only in deference to the decree of Pope Clement VIII (1592-1605), does one refrain from calling her a saint. But during the reigns of her father and brother she had lived so retired a life that the country at large knew little about her personally. If she was received with such wild enthusiasm as Queen, this was in large part because Northumberland had made himself so hated, though it was also because it was known that she would restore the Mass. Among the ruling classes she had the reputation not only of a spotless life but of an honesty so absolute that it sometimes seemed blunt and tactless. But though they were well aware that she had great strength of character—even to the point of obstinacy—they still thought she had let the conspirators off too lightly. The country had grown accustomed to blood-thirstiness under Henry VIII and then under the regimes of Somerset and Northumberland, and they were apprehensive of her mild disposition. Yet had she not made the ghastly mistake of the Spanish marriage, Mary's would have been a successful reign.

It is a truism that it is the bad kings who make history. Had it not been for the Spanish marriage and the persecution—the latter, it should be remembered, under a law passed by Parliament—Mary's reign would have been quite uneventful. She was all for a quiet life and for keeping England at peace with France and Scotland. She addressed herself to paying off the debts of her father and brother—or the debts incurred in the name of Edward VI—to giving an honest value to the coinage debased by Henry VIII (and debased much more by Northumberland), and to keeping on good terms with her neighbors. She might even have succeeded in what was dearest to her heart, the restoration of a complete Catholicism. This would have meant no revolution, but rather a check to the revolution which began with her father's infatuation with Anne Boleyn.

But very soon there was alarm, and an immense diminution of her popularity when it became virtually certain that Queen Mary was going to marry Prince Philip of Spain, the son of the Emperor Charles V. Most Englishmen would have preferred to see another Englishman as her husband, and they had one picked out for her, young Edward Courtenay, the son of the Marquis of Exeter whom Henry VIII had beheaded in 1538, partly to revenge himself upon Exeter's cousin, Cardinal Pole, but perhaps even more to extirpate all those of Plantagenet blood. Since boyhood, Edward Courtenay had been held in the Tower for safe-keeping. If he was a good deal younger than Mary, so also was Philip, and Courtenay's youth seemed the best guarantee of an heir to the throne, a "mere Englishman." The Cardinal himself was also spoken of as a possible husband for Mary, and that he was a Cardinal was only a slight obstacle, as so far he was merely in Deacon's orders, easily dispensable.* Though in Pole's case the discrepancy in age was the other way round, when Mary came to the throne Pole was only fifty-three, not too old to beget a child, or several children, supposing that Mary, now about thirty-eight, could conceive them. But Pole had already shown himself to be without ambition, when he virtually refused the papacy in the conclave of 1549; after that he was hardly likely to seek to become King of England. He was a quiet, aristocratic scholar, and he found celibacy much to his taste.

Most of the trouble arose from the fact that Mary, as was natural, asked her cousin the Emperor for advice, and the Emperor, as was natural, was seeking his own political advantage. Charles himself blundered badly, for it would have been much better for him—even on political grounds—to have sought to retain the friendship of England rather than

* For that matter, some years later when a Jesuit Cardinal, who was a priest, inherited the throne of Poland, his vows were dispensed with for the good of the Church.

create a marriage alliance. At any rate that would have been so in the long-run. But Charles could think only of the immediate advantage, and, after thinking for a moment of proposing himself as his cousin Mary's husband, he eventually strongly recommended his son. To Mary the offer seemed glittering, for though Philip would almost certainly not be elected Emperor in succession to his father, he would become King of Spain and the enormous Spanish dominions in the New World, of Naples and of the Low Countries. With such a husband she could count upon being safe from any attack by France, and, best of all, use Spanish power to help effect the dream of her life, a Catholic restoration.

Mary lost no time in making it clear that she would not entertain the thought of Courtenay, though Chancellor Gardiner, who had been with Courtenay in the Tower, argued in his favor until the Queen sharply silenced him. As for Cardinal Pole, he put himself out of the running and advised Mary to remain in her single state. Pole was especially opposed to her marrying Philip, sharing the all but universal sentiments of his fellow-countrymen—one might almost say *all* with the exception of those the Emperor bribed. Cranmer, as he was no longer a member of the Council, was not consulted, but naturally he was against the Spanish marriage for reasons of his own. He cannot be blamed in any way for what happened.

Cranmer of course thought that a marriage to Philip would overthrow his own work, but Gardiner, much more shrewdly, saw that to bring Philip into England as King-consort would make Catholicism seem like a Spanish importation, or give Protestant controversialists a chance to make a charge that was bound to be damaging—to the Holy See as well as to Mary herself. But Mary flared up, so that

Gardiner could only shrug his shoulders and let matters take their own course. There was no use arguing with a woman, least of all a woman like Mary—not about a question of this sort.

Gardiner never wanted the Marian persecution, thinking that the ancient heresy laws sufficed, and that even they should as a rule be held merely *in terrorem*. It was noticed that when the burnings did begin, none occurred in Gardiner's large diocese of Winchester. This was (at least in part) because few heretics were found there. On the other hand, Bishop Bonner of London—Foxe's "Bloody Bonner" —burned more than half of the martyrs, because London and the adjacent counties contained most of those who, as the law stood, deserved burning. But even Foxe admits that, though Bonner's manner was rough, he was a kindly sort of person. He got many of the heretics to recant, and some he employed for a month or two as gardeners, or in other capacities, while he tried his persuasive powers upon them.

Philip appears to have little to do with the matter, for though an *auto da fé* was frequent in Spanish territories,* the Emperor advised Mary to use a different method in England, in the beginning actually suggesting that she should not introduce changes in religion. And when the persecution did begin, Philip's chaplain, the Dominican Alphonso à Castro, went so far as to preach against it at court, which must have been with Philip's knowledge and approval. Mary herself was too soft-hearted to initiate persecution, and though there were some strong Catholics on the Council, they did not have enough political experience

---

* Even at an *auto da fé,* the majority of those who took part merely made an act of submission to the Church; but many were burned.

to have any influence worth talking about. The execution of the Act of Parliament was in the hands of Councilors who had served under Edward (in a few instances under Henry, too), and these men seldom had any very definite religious convictions. With them the persecution was merely a policy, for nearly all were quick to declare themselves Protestants under Elizabeth. They took good care that none of their own social standing went to the stake. Richard Rich is a case in point: after trapping St. John Fisher with lying promises and sending St. Thomas More to the block by perjury, and being Lord Chancellor under Somerset in 1548, he distinguished himself under Mary by his zeal for burning Protestants, reverting again to Protestantism under Elizabeth. Perhaps nobody was quite as base as this man, but he was only the worst of many time-servers. Their sole justification is that they thought severity was necessary if order was to be preserved. These were the men mainly responsible for the Marian persecution.

Cardinal Pole, though the Pope's Legate, was kept out of England until the Holy See had given guarantees that expropriators of monastic lands would not have to restore them. The idealistic Pole did not like this at all—it looked too much like a "deal." He realized, of course, that monastic property had already been so broken up, passing through many hands, that it was not feasible to make restitution, except in isolated cases; but he wished the Pope's guarantee to come as a free gift, after his Legate had been admitted. But the other method was simpler; many good enough Catholics were determined not to disgorge, even when it would have been possible to do so.

Cranmer must have looked at such things with cynical amusement. He did not understand his own danger, though he knew that Cardinal Pole was to be the new Archbishop of Canterbury. However, Cranmer was not formally deprived until a few days before his execution in 1556. Following Mary's accession, a formula of recantation in very general terms probably would have been accepted, but this could hardly be considered adequate after the appearance of Cranmer's manifesto.

He could have gone abroad, and one can believe that broad hints were dropped to that effect. As he was showing himself obdurate, he was transferred from house imprisonment at Lambeth Palace to the Tower. The suggestion that he retire on a pension was dropped. Wyatt's rebellion equated heresy and treason even in the minds of people indifferent to theology. It even promptly brought to the block the Queen's young cousin, Lady Jane Grey and her husband, whom Mary had quite intended to spare. But though Cranmer himself had been at least technically guilty of treason, and had been sentenced to death in 1553, it was well known that he was by disposition submissive to whoever it was that ruled. He therefore had some reason to hope that he would not be further molested.

Chapter Seventeen

The Trial at Oxford

It might be thought there was no need for Cranmer to be tried at all, and, indeed, though there was a trial—two, in fact—at Oxford, the main judgment passed upon him was at Rome. There it could only be decided (as the matter admitted no doubt) that Cranmer was a heretic; but no sentence of punishment could be passed other than of a purely ecclesiastical sort. In England, where Cranmer's heresy was still more manifest—or had been soon after little Edward ascended the throne—he was subject to the law, which made him liable to be burned at the stake. This, however, could only be done after competent ecclesiastical authority had passed on his case. Then, if proven guilty and if remaining obdurate, he would be handed over to the secular arm.

The trial as conducted by the church court was eminently fair and thorough. But it was hardly needed, so manifest to everybody in England had Cranmer's heresy been since at least 1548. The main objection must be that the punishment was inflicted by the Council, few of whose members had any genuine religious conviction. The only extenuating circumstance is that these men believed religious orthodoxy was necessary for social stability, and that, of course, it was clearly their duty to uphold.

This may be conceding too much. A suspicion arises that they persecuted as a means of parading beliefs that they did not hold, or that they held in a very loose grasp. Though

William Cecil was not a member of the Council, the Council gave him some employment, and he was able to swing on the flying trapeze with the greatest of ease. One of his descendants, that admirable writer Algernon Cecil, was to say of him that to have twice professed himself a Catholic and twice a Protestant was a bit too much.* A still darker suspicion is that to some of these men persecution was a means of ensuring their title to the bits of looted monastic property that had fallen to them. Up to the reign of James II the fear—a quite baseless one—persisted that they might be told to disgorge. But if they proved their orthodoxy by sending heretics to the stake, they thought they had a better chance of being left undisturbed in their possession of ill-gotten gains. All this, though the Pope himself had guaranteed that they would not be asked to make restitution. Yes, but that was Paul III; there was no telling what one of his successors might not take into his head to do.

According to John Foxe—who was a bit inclined to "pad" his accounts—about 270 people were burned. Some were arrested on a charge of felony, only to have the fact of their heresy accidentally emerge afterwards. Even so, the persecution was not only horrible in itself, but a horrible mistake, for it did more than anything else to bring on a wave of anti-Catholicism which has lasted to this day. Moreover, our disgust is increased by the fact that, with the exception of a few prominent ecclesiastics (Cranmer, of course, being by far the most important) all the martyrs were poor, simple and ignorant folk. Many were persuaded to recant; others recanted as soon as they smelled the fire; but there remained a number whose fortitude one cannot but admire, even if

* This was in his brilliantly written *A House in Bryanston Square*.

they were driven forward by fanaticism, or sometimes, it would seem, in a kind of hysteria.

Furthermore, a large proportion of the martyrs should, under the principles laid down by Canon Law, never have been burned at all, for the simple reason that they never were Catholics. Even while Henry VIII was on the throne, the constant denunciations of the Pope, to which everybody was subjected, had weakened the faith of many, indeed the faith of all except the most firmly grounded. And since then a new generation had come into being. Young people born between 1547 and (say) 1556 may have had a Catholic childhood, but had forgotten it. It was no more fair to punish them for heresy than it would be for warships manned by Christians to descend upon some heathen island in the South Pacific and put all its inhabitants to the sword as unbelievers. That may be the Moslem way; it is not, or should not be, the Catholic way. However, it must never be forgotten that everybody in Europe at that time took the attitude that heresy was the most appalling of crimes and should be punished fittingly—with death. It is one of the greatest ironies of history that Queen Mary, who was centuries ahead of her time in this matter (one may conjecture it was because of what she had learned from More's *Utopia,* which we positively know she studied in youth), should have been forced by circumstances to behave in such a way that most people still think her chief claim to fame is her bloody intolerance.

One cannot say of Thomas Cranmer, however, that he had never been a Catholic. Unless there was a sly secretiveness about him, he was, at least until 1530 (when he was about forty), a man of ordinary Catholic beliefs—perhaps lax, and very probably only practicing, even after his priesthood, in the routine fashion which was all too general then, and which is by no means unknown now. But he definitely was a Catholic, and though there may have been a gradual drift towards what we now call Protestantism, it was so slow as hardly to be noticeable—maybe even by himself—until he was in his late fifties. His was an almost excessively slow and cautious mind; and even at the end he has to be regarded as a moderate man compared, for example, with John Hooper, and even Hooper can be styled moderate when set beside some of the wilder and more eccentric men.

It must be granted that Cranmer stood for something that to him seemed of the greatest importance, though to us it is not easily comprehended. That was, the royal supremacy in matters of religion. That is why, even while desperately trying to save his own life, each of his last recantations contained some conditional phrase (usually as concealed as was possible) by which he sought to safeguard his central principle. The lack of complete candor was his personal undoing—in the sense that this brought his doom upon him—but, understood in its proper light, it was intended to preserve his intellectual honor. The dramatic circumstances of his death show not only that he was determined to cling to his beliefs, but that he could die not merely with fortitude but with a defiant flourish. Cranmer's martyrdom probably did as much to root Protestantism in England as the beautiful cadences of his Book of Common Prayer.

Other bishops—such as Ridley and Hooper and the ex-bishop Latimer—could be dealt with by the ordinary tribunals, though Ridley and Latimer were tried when Cranmer himself was tried the first time. But Cranmer's case was something special: it was referred to the Holy See, and though the Pope and his consistory could see plainly enough that Cranmer was a heretic, he was told (as a matter of form) to present himself in Rome within eighty days. This the English government did not permit, having, perhaps, the excuse that Roman tribunals are notoriously slow to act, but it was, nevertheless, not very fair. As against this it may be said that the government felt no need to send Cranmer to Rome to discover whether or not he was a heretic: nobody has ever questioned that he was, for those who share his beliefs are themselves obviously heretical—that is, according to all Catholic standards.

The suggestion has sometimes been made that Cranmer was executed because Reginald Pole wished to become Archbishop of Canterbury. Nothing could be further from the truth. Why should he have hankered for this position when he could have become Pope, or King of England? Even his cardinalate had practically to be forced upon him in 1537. He was the least ambitious of men; in fact, he would not accept either ordination or consecration until after Cranmer was dead—and then (as concerns consecration) reluctantly and because he could more effectively act as Papal Legate if he was also the Primate of England.

We might remember that the Marian heresy law did pass Parliament—which acted with unprecedented promptitude in the matter, when at last it was presented—and immediately afterwards the persecution began, with John Rogers, as Foxe somewhat quaintly puts it, "breaking the ice" at Smithfield. However, the persecution was not continuous; after the first executions there was a lull, which strongly suggests that it was hoped there would be no need for more. Indeed, there were several such periods during which the burnings stopped, for it was expected that those which had occurred would prove a sufficient deterrent. Nobody enjoyed what was going on, but everybody, except active heretics, admitted that it was a necessity—an unfortunate necessity.

On October 1, 1555, Ridley, Latimer, and of course Cranmer himself, were tried together; and fifteen days later Cranmer, from the roof of his prison, the Bocardo, saw Ridley and Latimer being led to the stake in the ditch by Balliol College. He could not have heard brave old Latimer urging Ridley to be of good cheer, as by God's grace they would that day light in England a candle that should never be put out. Even had the grand words been shouted at the top of Latimer's voice they could not have reached Cranmer; he was there to witness their burning (at a distance) in the hope that it would break down his own obstinacy. It might be remarked that—as was commonly done—bags of gunpowder were slung around their necks. Unnecessary cruelty was avoided wherever possible.

It was one of the rules of the game that a recantation, even if made at the stake itself, brought pardon; so it might seem that Cranmer was not fairly handled. Probably any of the statements he made would have been favorably received had it come from anybody but the Archbishop of Canterbury, or even from him promptly—for we know that many who were sentenced escaped the stake by making a withdrawal in most general terms. But because of his high office, and still more because of the part he had played in imposing Protestantism upon England, something very explicit had to be obtained from this exalted personage. He should have understood as much himself, but again—with his lack of the sense of reality—he seems to have thought that a perfunctory formula, or even hedging, would suffice.

What should be noted is that he was given every possible chance. Had Queen Mary been motivated by vindictiveness, she would have demanded that he be burned with Ridley and Latimer. But no, when one recantation was unsatisfactory, he was asked to make another—after theological experts had explained to him just what was wanted. So far from there being a settled determination to burn Cranmer, there was a hope that he would extricate himself. But he could do so only by being absolutely unequivocal. Instead he displayed a shiftiness which, while it may have indicated an intellectual dignity in the hidden recesses of his mind, created a very unfavorable impression upon the Queen and her Council. The extraordinary thing is the patience they showed.

Yet they blundered, and very badly. The new Catholic regime had obtained immense additional prestige in 1553 from the full and forthright recantation made by the Duke of Northumberland—spoken in public, too—the day before he was beheaded. They hoped to get something of the same sort from Cranmer, and had they obtained it, Protestantism would have been completely discredited. But even without getting just what they wanted, they would have been wise to accept one of his recantations—let us say the fourth—as meeting their requirements, even though it really did not. Of course they never had any idea what a grand concluding performance Cranmer was to put on; and, though this made his martyrdom a hundred times more effective, even apart from that dramatic flourish it was foolish to send him to the stake. There he snatched from them all, and much more, than had been offered by Northumberland.

The Archbishop of Canterbury was well housed, as befitted his eminence, in the Bocardo prison, but later was for a time given very pleasant entertainment by the Dean of Christ Church, the idea being to see what kindness would effect. When he spoke at his trials he was courteously heard, and even treated with deference. He was afforded enough freedom of debate to make some telling points. After all, he had been a professor of theology at Cambridge. But there he had used Latin, and the Scholastic mode, and in both he had grown a bit rusty. Nevertheless he was now obliged to use the syllogistic method of his early days, and it must be admitted that he carried the matter well, some might even say brilliantly, under the circumstances.

When Cranmer had his first trial, in company with Ridley and Latimer, his proculator was Doctor Weston. Weston declared that his purpose was the confutation of heretics, and Cranmer reasonably answered that, in that event, the conclusion was foreclosed. The gibe went round that Latimer leaned on Cranmer and Cranmer on Ridley. There was this much substance to it: Latimer was an old man, and was never much of a theologian, but rather would be called today a social reformer. Cranmer's interests were wider, but he did rely on Ridley, and, in fact, had reached his position under Ridley's guidance.

Cranmer, though a Cambridge man, was extended Oxford's courtesies, for a day or two later he was invited to take part in a disputation with John Harpsfield who was up for his D.D. degree. This debate was of course of an academic sort, and Dr. Weston who presided, paid the following compliment to Cranmer, "Your wonderful gentle behavior and modesty, is worthy of much commendation; and that I may not deprive you of your right and just deserving, I give you most hearty thanks in my own name, and in that of all my brethren." Upon which all present raised their university caps. Of course all this had no bearing on the trial, but it does indicate that Professor Pollard is wide of the mark in saying that Mary considered herself as "making a burnt-offering acceptable to God." It is hardly necessary to say that such an idea would have been utterly abhorrent to any Catholic, as it would have been to Pollard himself.

In Rome, when Cranmer did not answer the summons to appear within eighty days, he was pronounced contumacious and accordingly excommunicated, which was not very fair, as the English government did not permit him to go to Rome. The only justification possible is that his heresy had been notorious for years, so the condemnation was merely a formality. The Prefect of the Inquisition, however, delegated Bishop James Brooks of Gloucester to hear what Cranmer had to say, associating with him the Dean of St. Paul's and the Archdeacon of Canterbury. When Cranmer was brought before these judges, he refused to recognize their authority—as they represented the Holy See—but accepted the counsel for the prosecution, Drs. Martin and Story. In other words he recognized the royal but not the papal authority.

Dr. Story, a layman, deserves a word because he had been Chancellor to Bishop Bonner and was a Member of Parliament. Upon the accession of Elizabeth he refused to take the oath of conformity, but made his way to the Low Countries, where he was naturalized. It was a mark against him that he had advocated the establishment of the Inquisition at Antwerp, but under no circumstances did this justify his being kidnaped there and, upon being brought to England, made to suffer a traitor's appalling death at Tyburn. In Cranmer's case his sentence accorded with the English law; Queen Elizabeth acted towards Story in total disregard of international law.

At this late date it would be tedious to recount Cranmer's trial at length.* It was common knowledge that he was a heretic, and a traitor besides, though he was not being tried for treason, of which offense he had, in effect, been pardoned. But regarding other matters he declared that nobody had been so reluctant to accept a bishopric as he had been (though even undue ambition would not have been a punishable crime), and he did deny that the works written during the reign of Edward VI really were by him. Quite openly he said in court: "I will never consent that the Bishop of Rome shall have any jurisdiction within this realm." The paradoxical position he advanced has been put by the Anglican C. H. Smyth in his *Cranmer and the Reformation under Edward VI:* "He died for the Royal Supremacy in defiance of the Crown." Smyth more fully than anybody else expounds the development of Cranmer's views regarding the Sacrament of the Altar. Cranmer had once, as he admitted, believed in Transubstantiation, but had gradually under the influence of Bucer and Ridley reached what is called "Soumerverianism," a term which will be incomprehensible to most people. He may for a while have dallied with Consubstantiation, though Lutheranism never obtained much foothold in England. Nor did Zwinglianism nor Calvinism very deeply affect him. What he held, as Smyth explains, was that "the reception of the bread and wine may be accompanied by a special kind of experience on the part of the soul: yet only when the soul is qualified or adapted therefor by its own condition." While it may not be quite fair to describe this, as Cardinal Gasquet and Edmund

* This may be found in the *Memorials of Cranmer,* Parker Society, pp. 12, 50, 391, 430. This matter was taken from the 1583 edition of Foxe, and has been used in detail over and over again.

Bishop have done, as "the Real Absence," it is clear that the "Presence" in the Cranmerian sense was wholly subjective. Possibly the majority of present day Protestants are Soumerverian without knowing it; more probably the majority treat Holy Communion as hardly more than a commemoration of the Last Supper. It is that, too, even to Catholics, as the words of the Latin Mass make perfectly clear, but it is also a great deal more than that. By orthodox Lutherans themselves Cranmer would have to be regarded as a thoroughgoing heretic.

One of the points raised by Story was that Cranmer had committed perjury by giving notice beforehand to a select group that he would not consider himself bound by the oath he took to the Pope. It might be urged in Cranmer's defense that Henry VIII compelled this perjury, but while this may lessen Cranmer's guilt, it was perjury none the less. But again, this was only a minor point; Cranmer was burnt for heresy, and he made many admissions at the trial itself, so that, under the law as it stood, he was guilty up to his eyebrows. The perjury, however, raised the question whether Cranmer was a man ever to be trusted, which was one reason why the Council demanded a complete submission, instead of the formal sort of recantation which might have been accepted from another man. In addition there were Cranmer's controversial writings, his Forty-two Articles and, not least, his Book of Common Prayer. In this last case it was beside the point that he had proved himself a great writer of English prose.

The very full and explicit recantation of the Duke of Northumberland on the day before his execution naturally made a deep impression in favor of the Church. Now if only Cranmer could be brought to do something along the same lines, it was thought that the Protestant cause in England would be given a blow from which it could hardly survive. Indeed, at the beginning of Mary's reign Protestantism was brought very low, reviving only because of the hated Spanish marriage and, to a lesser degree, because of the revulsion of feeling due to the persecutions. But the unknown future lay largely in English hands. Had it not been for the prestige that a Protestant England eventually obtained, Lutheranism would almost certainly have come to be regarded as a quaint opinion entertained along the shores of the Baltic. As we know, Calvinism was destined to gradual obsolescence, despite the force and clarity of John Calvin's mind. If only England had permanently remained Catholic, an immense prestige would have lain in Catholic hands, instead of the position being reversed. That this happened was largely due to the martyrdom of Thomas Cranmer.

Not only to his martyrdom, of course. Though it was the headstrong Henry VIII who broke with the Roman obedience, it was the mild Cranmer, more than any other man, who constructed the Church of England. Had Cranmer not been available, Somerset and Northumberland would have found somebody else, but someone not nearly so well adapted to their purpose. Fanatics would have fallen out with one another and brought confusion, if not disaster upon their entire cause. It was the relative moderation and instinctive seemliness of Cranmer that gave the Dukes' enterprises some degree of stability. Now he had to make the most complete retractation. Nothing less would serve, coming from him.

This was all the more necessary because of the defiance Cranmer had shown in his trial before Bishop Brooks. Yet, to extract the submission demanded proved far from easy. The first retractions were so brief and perfunctory as to seem contemptuous. This strongly suggests that not so much as a hint of the possibility of pardon had been given Cranmer. But after he had witnessed the burning of Ridley and Latimer from the roof of his prison in the Bocardo, his mind was seized with panic. Until his fourth recantation he had used formulas that almost any heretic would have readily signed: he merely affirmed that he believed all the articles of the Christian religion and Catholic faith, as the Catholic Church believes and always has believed. In short, he held the primitive faith and only rejected the incrustations, though about these "incrustations" he was prudent enough to say nothing.

New tactics were now employed, for in February, 1556, he was transferred to the comfortable house of the Dean of Christ Church, and though he was not given untrammeled freedom, he received every kindness, and enjoyed good food and pleasant company. Now perhaps he would break down. And so he did, to some extent, writing a much longer retraction in Latin, professing to believe the Pope the Supreme Head of the Roman Church, to believe in Transubstantiation and six other Sacraments. But while admitting the existence of Purgatory, he touched very lightly on the efficacy of Mass for departed souls. This recantation, however, made everything hinge upon his submission to Philip and Mary, implying that everything that had gone before had been written at their request. The witnesses to this deed are Henry Syddall, one of the Canons of Christ Church, and Juan de Villa Garcina, a Spanish Dominican who had been deputed to persuade Cranmer of his errors.

As that retractation was not considered quite satisfactory

either, Garcina went to work again and, in part, got the
following out of Cranmer: * "I, Thomas Cranmer, formerly
Archbishop of Canterbury, confess and mourn from my
heart that I have grievously offended against Heaven and
the realm of England, nay against the universal Church of
Christ, which I have persecuted more cruelly than once did
Paul, who was also a blasphemous and contumelious per-
secutor. Moreover, may I, who have surpassed Saul in my
malice and wickedness, be able to make good as Paul did
that which I detracted from Christ and the use of the
Church." (Unfortunately even here Cranmer has to bring
in his formula about his Sovereign.) However, he confesses
himself deserving of "not human and temporal but of divine and eternal punishment" and to be unworthy of any
benefice or kindness "because I sinned grievously against
King Henry VIII and especially against his wife Katharine
when I made myself the cause and author of that divorce
which since was the root of all the calamities which have
come upon the kingdom. Hence the death of so many,
hence schism in the whole kingdom, hence heresies, hence
the destruction of so many bodies and souls as hardly could
I set down the tale." This raises some suspicion that he
was trying to placate Queen Mary and that he thought his
principle offense was what he did in the matter of the divorce. However, he goes on more amply to confess what he
has done regarding heresies "in which I was myself the
chief teacher and leader." And he declares that what most
troubles his mind is what he has done with regard to the
Blessed Sacrament, "denying the Body and Blood of Christ
to be really and truly contained under the species of Bread

* I adopt the translation given on pp. 317–9 of Belloc's *Cranmer*.

and Wine." (The word "contained," artfully slipped in, will connote to a theologian something less than Transubstantiation.) But he goes on to deplore that "I have defrauded the souls of the dead from the benefit of the most exalted Sacrifice," a few lines later praying "the Serene Sovereigns of England and Spain, Philip and Mary, that with royal clemency they also will forgive me," again making matters hinge on royal authority.

One is very sorry for Cranmer, as he was trying to go as far as he could without stultifying himself completely. But he must have known that theologians would weigh every word of this and find a good deal of significance in what he omitted. Even so, had this been written by anybody else, it would almost certainly have been accepted. As it was, Cranmer did not hear what final decision had been made about his fate. That is hardly fair, for though he received no official word that he was to be burned, Garcina probably explained just what was wanted from him and, without making any promises, encouraged him to hope.

The ceremony of degradation was performed by Bishops Bonner and Thirlby before the high altar of Christ Church Cathedral. Bonner had been appointed a Bishop by Henry VIII, but he refused to accept the Edwardian changes in religion and so was imprisoned for years and reinstated in London only after Mary's accession. But Thirlby had been suspected of being a Romanist at heart, though he was one of Cranmer's protégés. While he by no means relished this commission of helping to degrade Cranmer, Bonner entered into it with vigor, not because he felt any personal animosity against Cranmer, but because it was in his own diocese of London that heretics most abounded, and he had the best of reasons for knowing what harm the man had done.

Now Cranmer, dressed in canvas vestments—those of deacon, priest and archbishop—and still wearing his pallium, and with crozier in hand had them pulled off him. He did not seem to mind it very much that Bonner was unnecessarily rough, until his pallium was taken. Then he did vehemently protest, and his crozier had to be wrested away by main force. After this his fingers were given a ritual scraping with a pin to show that he was no longer capable of saying Mass, the Mass he had said a thousand times, as lately as 1548, since which date he had done his best to uproot it in England. What happened that day did not make a pleasant scene, and none of the participants could have relished it.

When he was lodged in the house of the Dean of Christ Church, he enjoyed his stay and went about telling people that his heart was now glad because he was back in the Catholic Faith. Yet when he met Garcina he was still inclined to hang onto a few reservations, though perhaps he should be credited with sincerity, in which there may have been only a pinch of slyness. In the Catholic atmosphere of Christ Church, Catholic sentiments revived, and he went to confession and Holy Communion, though now of course only as a layman. (One wonders how, in view of his Papal excommunication, unless this had been removed by the Ordinary.)

Hope was renewed that Thomas Cranmer would now really be a Catholic for what remained to him of life. He was about sixty. There might be ample time for him to do much towards the undoing of his work, especially the work of the past eight years. There could be no question of letting him act as a bishop again, but it might have been possible to appoint him to a minor benefice or to retire him on a pension. In any event, he would naturally have been expected to appear before the public from time to time and make it unmistakeably clear that the arch-heretic had been converted. But suspicions about him seem to have been aroused even during the Christ Church period—perhaps unjustifiably by an overzealous or stupid person—for he went back to the Bocardo. The Council knew him too well to trust him very far, but Mary was of a merciful disposition; otherwise he would have gone to the block in 1553.

This stay at Christ Church was for Cranmer not only a pleasant time, it was perhaps the happiest period of his whole life. One is glad that he had it, ghastly as was his end. He had begun to hope, no doubt encouraged in this by the Canons and Garcina, though none of them were authorized to hold out any hope, still less to make any promise. Then suddenly there arrived the order that he was to go back to the Bocardo. Even that could not be taken to mean that his execution had at last been decided upon, though it must have looked rather ominous. It may have meant only an intention to give a further twist of the screw, to see whether it was to Christ Church or the Catholic Church that Cranmer had been converted. But if this change did not mean a definite decision on the part of the Council, it seems an enormous error in judgment. The Bocardo could only have made the highly-strung old man nervous to no purpose. Perhaps if he had only been left in the custody of the Dean and the Canons, Cranmer's story would have had a different ending.

Chapter Eighteen

Into the Fire

There is every reason for believing that official word of what had been decided did not reach Cranmer until an hour or so before his execution. What Cranmer did know was that a great occasion was being prepared for March 21, 1556, when he was to stand on a platform in front of St. Mary's Church and make a public retractation. In preparation for this he had written out a speech to deliver. It contained much that was admirable, including a reproof of worldliness, an exhortation to obey Philip and Mary, and especially an appeal to be kind to the poor, but only in the last paragraph was there any real withdrawal: "I say and believe that our Saviour Jesus Christ is really and substantially contained in the Blessed Sacrament of the Altar, under the forms of bread and wine."

The official silence does not seem at all fair, though it is possible that Lord Williams of Thame, in charge of the affairs of the day, was told to consult Dr. Henry Cole, the Provost of Eton, who was to preach the sermon and who had been given wide discretionary powers, and that they decided Cranmer had not dealt adequately with matters to the immediate point. There may have been a bare chance that Cranmer would still avoid the stake. When Cranmer knew at last what decision had been reached, he was furiously angry. Who shall blame him? This was not according to the rules of the game.

The occasion reminds one of a Spanish *auto da fé,* a public ceremony at which most of the condemned recanted. Cranmer sat in tears with his face in his hands, so that those who saw him believed his repentance genuine. As the day was windy and stormy, the proceedings had to be in the church building. Cranmer joined the procession, apparently still in the expectation that his life would be spared.

Cole presumably had seen Cranmer's prepared speech in advance, but we do not positively know. We do know that the Provost of Eton presented a list of Cranmer's chief offenses but admitted that what he had done in the matter of the divorce might have sprung from compulsion rather than malice. At last Cole came to the main point: "Never had evils so enormous been excused, never had a man continuing in them been pardoned, and for the sake of example pardon could not now be granted: the Queen and Council had taken their decision and Cranmer was to die." But Cranmer should have been told about this in time to prepare for death. In any event, repentant heretics had, with one or two doubtful exceptions, always been pardoned, until, under Henry VIII's Act of Six Articles (which had been repealed in 1548), everyone who denied Transubstantiation was made food for the flames, however completely he renounced his heresy. That clause had only now and then been enforced, largely because Cranmer had co-operated with Cromwell to nullify the law. The understanding under Mary was that retractation would be accepted.

Gardiner himself had no responsibility for the burning, for though he was alive at the time of Cranmer's first trial (in 1555) he was in poor health and died before the year was out. Then Cardinal Pole was offered the Chancellorship but refused it; he would not even accept a seat in the

Council. However, as Cranmer's was a case of heresy, Pole did have some correspondence with the Holy See about it. But Pole had shown himself a mild man in England, preferring, as Foxe remarks, to burn the body of a disinterred heretic rather than send a live one to the stake. Yet Mary no doubt sought his advice, and in a dispassionate way he may have thought the burning of so notorious a heretic would be a salutary warning. Also, when Pole read Cranmer's series of retractations, he must have observed that there was always something slyly omitted, or slyly slipped in, which destroyed their value. But Pole was certainly not cruel; indeed, when in 1538 the Pope made him Administrator of the Papal States, the English Cardinal was severely criticized in some quarters for being much too mild.

One may suspect Cranmer of playing for time in giving a long series of recantations. Mary's health was known to be poor, and Cranmer may have known that Elizabeth, who was sure to be Mary's successor, was to say the least, no Catholic fanatic. While the days of the prim, puritanical Edward would be unlikely to return, nevertheless Elizabeth's accession would be sure to change the picture completely. It would probably even mean that Cranmer would be reinstated as Archbishop of Canterbury.

Nevertheless, even to suggest this may be very unfair to Cranmer, a man who took little or no interest in politics. He could hardly eat his words and expect to retain the good opinion of the nation. Almost certainly Cranmer was trying to find a formula which would be acceptable to the Council, and yet not be too stultifying to himself. For this he can hardly be blamed, though it would have been better had he been forthright and explicit from the start. But this was not in his nature; he had long been walking a tightrope and the thing had become a habit.

Yet there had been grave imprudences in the man's life. One was his marriage in youth to the barmaid Black Joan, which meant the loss of his college Fellowship, something that only her early death restored. Then, as a priest, while on a diplomatic mission in Germany, he had again married. (Perhaps in both instances the lady in the case had virtually seduced him, so that he was only doing what was hardly possible to avoid.) Then, at the beginning of Mary's reign, there was that truculent manifesto, whether or not he meant it for the general public. Finally, at his trials at Oxford, he had been very outspoken, showing that he had a fearless side to his rather strange character. It was as though a mouse had suddenly changed into a lion.

In his last hour on earth—his last twenty minutes in fact—the leonine Cranmer appeared again.

Cole in his sermon at St. Mary's told the weeping old man before him that he had done glory to God by his penitence, and now was to go to his heavenly home. He promised that in every church in Oxford a Mass would be said for him, and every priest present was asked to say a Mass for the repose of Cranmer's soul. All were deeply moved, and all were praying for one so soon to die. Those who formerly had hated him as a heretic now loved him for his return to the Faith. There was no malice in any heart. Even those on the Council who had voted against pardoning him were sincerely sorry for a man whom all of them had known and liked.

Cranmer, still in tears, rose to speak after Cole had ended. Then he read part of his prepared speech, but did not get as far as the last sentence, the only one containing anything that resembled a recantation.* One is left with the impression that that was meant to be an extemporaneous but definite recantation should Cole have announced his pardon. As Cole did the opposite, Cranmer concluded in a rage: "I see before mine eyes presently either Heaven ready to receive me, or Hell ready to swallow me up. I shall, therefore, today show you my very faith; for now is no time to dissemble, whatever I have written in times past." There was one thing that troubled his conscience more than anything he ever did: he had written to save his life, if possible. With this he publicly repudiated his recantations. "And forasmuch as I have written many things contrary to what I believe in my heart, my hand shall first be punished; for if I may come to the fire it shall first be burned. And as for the Pope, I refuse him, for Christ's enemy and anti-Christ, with all his false doctrine." There Cranmer is at last plain.

We should not object that the bit about the hand is false dramatics. Cranmer was little addicted to the dramatic, but at that moment he should be excused on the ground of being overwrought. Of course it was not his hand that had offended in any way, but his head and heart. In an execution, the offending part is not burned first. The words were not logical, but they were the right words for obtaining dramatic effect, and that moment was, above everything else, dramatic.

Even if Cranmer had an inkling of what was going to happen when he was told at the Bocardo that morning to wear nothing except his nightshirt, he still seems to have gone to St. Mary's with the intention of dying repentant, as many

* *Miscellaneous Writings and Letters of Thomas Cranmer,* Parker Society, 1846, p. 566.

other condemned men had died, until he was swept by other feelings. But he may have continued to hope, even in his nightshirt; or this may have been an example of how slowly accumulated emotions might all at once come irresistibly to a head. His heresy had only very slowly—almost imperceptibly—developed over a number of years. Once developed, it was very powerful. The only chance of freeing him from it was to give him ample time in the delightful company of the Canons at Christ Church. This chance had been lost when he was sent back to the Bocardo.

Now that at last he knew his fate beyond any shadow of doubt, he had a right to consider himself badly treated. What the large congregation at St. Mary's saw was an old man, with a long straggly beard, rushing down the center aisle, then out into the rain towards the stake. Even there a man named Edge of Brazenose College begged him not to go to his death in such a disposition, but to make some declaration of his Catholic Faith. Cranmer's only answer was, "As for that recantation, I repent it right sore because I knew it was against the truth." If so, he had only been guilty of cowardice; we may hope that he was subjectively truthful. No man wants to die with a lie upon his lips.

Lord Williams of Thame, coming up, called out, "Make short! Make short!" We do not hear of any merciful bags of gunpowder hung on Cranmer, to make death more speedy, though there may have been. But it is certain that he did exactly as he said he would and kept his right hand in the rising flame. The astonishing gesture was intended to let everybody know that he died a Protestant.

Selected Bibliography

Selected Bibliography

Allen, J. W. *A History of Political Thought in the Sixteenth Century*. New York, 1928.

Armstrong, E. *The Emperor Charles V*, 2 vols. London, 1902.

Belloc, Hilaire. *Cranmer*. Philadelphia and London, 1931.

Brewer, J. S. *The Reign of Henry VIII*, 2 vols. London, 1884.

Bridgett, T. E., C.SS.R. *Life of Blessed John Fisher*, 2nd ed. London, 1922.

Burnet, Gilbert. *The History of the Reformation of the Church of England* (ed. by N. Pocock), 7 vols. Oxford, 1865.

Calendar of State Papers, Edward VI, Foreign.

Cardwell, E. *The Two Liturgies of Edward VI. Compared.* London, 1841.

——. *The Reformation of the Ecclesiastical Laws*, new ed. Oxford, 1850.

Chambers, R. W. *Thomas More*. London, 1935.

Cheney, E. P. *Social Changes in England in the Sixteenth Century*. Boston, 1895.

Chronicle of the Grey Friars of London (ed. J. G. Nichols). Camden Society, 1852.

Chronicle of Queen Jane and Queen Mary (ed. J. G. Nichols). Camden Society, 1850.

Constant, G. *The Reformation in England* (Vol. I. trans. by

R. E. Scantlebury. New York, 1934; Vol. II. trans. by E. I. Watkins, London, 1942).

Cranmer, Thomas. *The two editions of The Book of Common Prayer.* (This is included in the Everyman's Library.)

——. *Cranmer's Liturgical Projects,* ed. by J. Wickham Legg. Bradshaw Society, 1915.

——. *Liturgies of Edward VI,* ed. by J. Kettlery. Parker Society, 1844.

——. *Miscellaneous Letters and Writings,* ed. for the Parker Society by J. E. Cox. Cambridge, 1844, 1846.

——. *The Remains of Thomas Cranmer,* ed. by H. Jenkyns, 4 vols. Oxford, 1833.

Dictionary of National Biography.

Dixon, R. W. *The History of the Church of England from the Abolition of the Roman Jurisdiction,* rev. ed. in 6 vols. London, 1893.

Dodd, Charles (pseudonym for Hugh Tootel). *The Church of England from 1500 to 1688* (ed. by M. A. Tierney), 5 vols. London, 1839–1843.

Dodds, M. H. and R. *The Pilgrimage of Grace,* 2 vols. London, 1915.

Edward VI, King. *Literary Remains of Edward VI,* ed. by J. G. Nichols. Roxburghe Club, 1857.

Fisher, H. A. L. *The Political History of England* (Vol. V. 1485–1547) London, 1906.

Foxe, John. *Acts and Monuments* (ed. by J. Pratt), 8 vols. London, 1853–70.

Friedman, Paul. *Anne Boleyn,* 2 vols. London, 1884.

Froude, James Anthony. *The Reign of Henry VIII,* 3 vols; *The Reign of Edward VI; The Reign of Mary Tudor.* Everyman's Library, n.d.

Fuller, Thomas. *The Church History of Britain,* ed. by J. S. Brewer. Vols. II, III & IV. London, 1845.

Gairdner, James. *The English Church in the Sixteenth Century.* London, 1904.

——. *Lollardy and the Reformation in England,* 4 vols. London, 1908–13.

Gardiner, Stephen. *Letters,* ed. by J. A. Muller. London, 1933.

Garrett, Christina Hallowell. *The Marian Exiles.* Cambridge, 1938.

Gasquet, Aidan Cardinal. *Cardinal Pole and his Early Friends.* London, 1927.

——. *The Eve of the Reformation.* London, 1913.

——. *Henry VIII and the English Monasteries,* 2 vols. London, 1899.

—— (with Edmund Bishop). *Edward VI and the Book of Common Prayer.* London, 1891.

Green, Alice Stopford. *Town Life in the Fifteenth Century.* London, 1894.

Haile, Martin. *The Life of Reginald Pole.* New York, 1910.

Hall, Edward. *Chronicle,* ed. by Charles Whibley, 2 vols. London and Edinburgh, 1904.

Herbert of Cherbury, Lord. *The Life and Reign of King Henry the Eighth* (reprint from Kennet's folio ed. of 1719). London, 1872.

Heywood, J. *Early Cambridge University and College Estates.* London, 1855.

Innes, A. D. *England under the Tudors,* rev. by J. M. Henderson. London, 1932.

Latimer, Hugh. *Sermons.* Everyman's Library, n.d.

Legg, J. W. *Cranmer's Liturgical Projects.* Henry Bradshaw Society, 1915.

Letters and Papers, Foreign and Domestic, Henry VIII, ed. by J. S. Brewer, vols. 1 to 4; 5–13 by J. Gairdner; and 14–21 by J. Gairdner and R. H. Brodie, with *addenda.*

Lingard, John. *History of England,* ed. by Hilaire Belloc, Vol. V, New York, 1912.

Machyn, Henry. *Diary.* Camden Society, 1848.

Mackie, J. D. *The Earlier Tudors.* Oxford, 1952.

Maitland, F. W. *Roman Canon Law in the Church of England.* London, 1898.

Maitland, S. R. *Essays on Subjects Connected with the Reformation in England.* London, 1849.

Mattingley, Garret. *Catherine of Aragon.* Boston, 1941.

Maynard, Theodore. *Henry the Eighth.* Milwaukee, 1949.

——. *Queen Elizabeth* (abridged ed.). Milwaukee, 1954.

——. *The Crown and the Cross: a Biography of Thomas Cromwell.* New York, 1950.

——. *Bloody Mary,* Milwaukee, 1955.

Merriman, R. B. *Life and Letters of Thomas Cromwell,* 2 vols. Oxford, 1902.

Moorman, J. H. R. *A History of the Church of England.* New York, 1950.

Mozley, J. F. *John Foxe and his Book.* London, 1940.

Muller, J. A. *Stephen Gardiner and the Tudor Reaction.* London, 1926.

Mullinger, J. B. *The University of Cambridge,* 2 vols. Cambridge, 1873, 1911.

Narratives of the Reformation, ed. by J. G. Nichols. Camden Society, 1859.

Pickthorne, Kenneth. *Tudor Government,* 2 vols. Cambridge, 1934.

Pocock, Nicholas. "The Condition of Morals and Religious

Belief in the Reign of Edward VI." *English Historical Review*, X, 1895, pp. 417–444.

Pollard, A. F. *Thomas Cranmer*. New York and London, 1906.

——. *England under Protector Somerset*. London, 1900.

——. *The History of England from the Accession of Edward VI to the Death of Elizabeth* (Vol. VI of the *Political History of England*). London and New York, 1910.

Prescott, H. F. M. *A Spanish Tudor; The life of "Bloody Mary."* New York, 1940. (Reissued, with some revisions in 1953 as *Mary Tudor*.)

Rashdell, H. *The Universities of Europe in the Middle Ages*. Oxford, 1895.

Read, Conyers. *Bibliography of British History, Tudor Period, 1485–1603*. Oxford, 1933.

Rose-Throup, Francis. *The Western Rebellion of 1549*. London, 1913.

Schenck, W. Reginald. *Reginald Pole, Cardinal of England*. New York, 1950.

Smith, H. Maynard. *Henry VIII and the English Reformation*. New York, 1949.

Smith, L. B. *Tudor Prelates and Politics*. Princeton, N. J., 1953.

Smyth, G. H. *Cranmer & the Reformation under Edward VI*. Cambridge, 1926.

Stone, J. M. *The History of Mary Tudor, Queen of England*. London, 1901.

Strype, John. *Ecclesiastical Memorials*, 6 vols. Oxford, 1822.

——. *Memorials of the Most Reverend Father in God, Thomas Cranmer*, 2 vols., ed. by P. E. Barnes. London, 1853.

Thurston, Herbert, S. J. "The Canon Law of the Divorce," *English Historical Review*, XIX, 1904, pp. 632–645.

Todd, Henry John. *The Life of Archbishop Cranmer*, 2 vols. London, 1831.

Tytler, P. F. *England under the Reigns of Edward VI and Mary*, 2 vols. London, 1839.

White, Beatrice. *Mary Tudor*. London, 1935.

Williams, C. H. *The Making of Tudor Despotism*. London, 1928.